Visionary Women Leaders

Discovering the Greatness Within You

Visionary Women Leaders

Discovering the Greatness Within You

Range Sinikas Founder of World Conference and Awards

Introduction and Conclusion María Angélica Benavides, EdD, EdD

Editor Barb Swan-Wilson

Ragne Sinikas * María Angélica Benavides, EdD * Forbes Riley
Amber Ann Lyons * Barb Swan-Wilson * Carmen Franco * Cheryl Thibault
H.E. Desiree Richardson, DLA, DLITT *Diane Lang * Francesca Richardson, PhD.
* Helen Argyrou * Ingrid Vasiliu-Feltes, MD, EMBA *Khalilah Hunter-Johnson, PhD.
* Maria Renee Davila * Nontsikelelo 'Ntsiki' Ncoco * Rosalind L. Willis, PhD * Rochele Lawson
Sarifa Alonto-Younes, EdD * Vi Ho, DDS, MSD * Viola Edward De Glanville

Visionary Women Leaders

Discovering the Greatness Within You

Published by B-Global Publishing.

Copyright © 2022

This book may be purchased for educational, business, or promotional sales. Special discounts are available on quantity purchased by corporations, associations, and others. For more information or to order additional copies of this book, contact the publisher at the address above.

Orders by U.S. trade bookstores and wholesalers. Email supportstaff@drbglobal.net

B-Global Publishing brings authors to your live event. For more information or to book an event, contact supportstaff@drbglobal.net

Manufactured and printed in the United States of America distributed globally by

B-GlobalPublishing.com

Acknowledgements

We are dedicating this chapter to all the amazing visionary women leaders that dare to step into their greatness and write a chapter in this book. We also want to acknowledge all the visionary women willing and ready to step into their greatness. Remember, you have the courage, bravery, and vision to think bigger, take bigger steps, and achieve your desired empire.

We want to thank Barb Swan-Wilson for countless hours of editing and making sure the authors shared their message in a precise and clear way.

All the authors want to thank their husbands, partners, sons, daughters, and friends who supported them during their dark times and time away from home. 'Thank you for sticking to us like glue in good times and tough times. We could not step into our greatness without you believing in us and standing by us at all times.'

Thank you to all those who have boosted our spirits, motivated us, and given us very specific ideas, strategies, tools, and resources that built the empire we stand on today.

Thank you to the team who supported us by writing this book and making it happen. Your multiple edits and redos have helped create a masterpiece improving this book's impact and making an enormous difference.

Table of Contents

Introduction

by María Angélica Benavides, EdD

The Visionary Women Leaders: Discovering the Greatness Within purpose is to help Visionary Leaders Turn their Vision into Reality. We help women globally to see clearly and vividly so they can begin to communicate what the future holds. Visionary leaders anticipate what's coming, both opportunities and obstacles. Our main goal is to ensure the vision of other women becomes a reality by stating clear goals, outlining a strategic plan for achieving those goals, and equipping and empowering each member to take action on the plan at the organization, team, and individual levels. We want to aspire female leaders to step into their greatness and lead from a position of integrity, influence, innovation, and share amazing stories on how the greatest success is sometimes achieved in life challenges. The idea of greatness can be pretty intimidating for many. People reserve the idea of greatness for superheroes that history reveres or are on comic strips. In fact, we shy away from describing ourselves as great, but greatness is not something to shy away from. Many were born to be great. This greatness shows when you have a big vision. Your vision may not be accomplished in your life, but others are on board with you working to achieve your vision and will carry on with what you started. You need to know that visionary leaders create a vision bigger than themselves that other people want to follow.

"The two most important days in life are the day you were born and the day you discover the reason why." - Mark Twain

Once you are clear about why you were born and the contributions you want to make in the world, just do it!

We have a clear idea of how the future should look. We set out concrete steps to bring a vision to life, and then they lead a team of people in that direction.

The book builds on six central agreements the authors have in common:

1. Discovering the Greatness Within
2. Birthing Your Passion
3. Successful Caring, Connecting and Empowering
4. Innovation Approach
5. Elevating as a Global Visionary Leader
6. Generational Impact

This book idea started with several World Women Conference and Awards (WWCA) visionary leaders from around the world who have come together to energize and inspire women to work toward their future goals, harnessing the power of leadership and community to empower women to achieve their full potential. Ragne Sinikas is the WWCA founder and leader of this organization. Other fabulous ladies joined this book project to help impact and influence in a bigger way.

We aim to reach millions of women worldwide with our message to multiply our impact and contribution to the world. This book is not about making you a guru in the way most people have thought about it. We are not telling you how to be a visionary leader. But we want to inspire and motivate you to discover your greatness to gain the confidence and bravery to take the risk to become the best version of yourself. You are about to discover how 20 fabulous ladies took their challenges and used them as ammunition to do what it takes to be great. You have been told and programmed to think small and shrink. This book will encourage you to think big and create a big vision that will impact millions. You will read how these 20 women were inspired and motivated by other visionary leaders. The 20 phenomenal women will share their empowering results and how COVID-19 didn't become an obstacle but opened the doors to new opportunities to achieve greatness. These amazing women will share their greatest achievements. These achievements were not easy, but they show it is possible to achieve your ideas and dreams.

The Visionary Leaders in this book share strategies that worked for them to achieve their greatness level. We encourage women to join other great organizations or create their own community to expand, build strong relations, make stronger connections, and be surrounded by giants that will boost your spirit, inspire you, and get you up again when you fall. All these phenomenal women in the book encourage you to thrive and dare to dream big. Together we can impact millions! You are doing important work, and people need you out there in the world. Never give up. Join the industry of brilliant, compassionate, and visionary leaders so we can inspire and instruct others with advice and knowledge.

Discovering the Greatness Within

Chapter 1

Sustainable Empathic Leadership

Ragne Sinikas

The Founder of World Women Conference & Awards

Introduction

As a global marketer focused on helping brands go from presence to profit, Ragne's mission is to help every person realize and unlock their true potential. She believes that everyone has a powerful message that can help impact the world. Coupled with cutting-edge tools and technology, one can help accelerate this process through omnipresence. Every individual has the expertise, experience, knowledge, know-how, ideas, programs, services, and even a hobby that can be captured through amazing content and published to multiple platforms to impact others. When someone has a powerful message, life-changing expertise, or deep understanding of a hot topic, Ragne empowers them by teaching them to turn this wisdom into purpose-driven income streams online. What better than to turn their presence into profit leveraging their own knowledge.

Mission

Ragne is a global marketer focused on helping people and brands go from presence to profit. She empowers people through teaching to share their stories and knowledge. Then she releases these programs, services, and know-how ideas onto multiple platforms, sharing these powerful messages creating a positive impact on the world.

Mission Statement: To help every person realize and unlock their true potential, repositioning women for high performance, improved leadership, and strong participation in society's economic and social development.

Vision

Ragne Sinikas is an honorable woman in her community and around the world. She is a visionary and brings in the right people to complete a suitable task. She is full of love, strength, companionship, and caring. Everything that Ragne does has a true meaning and is changing lives globally. Ragne is helping South Africa with trying to bring electricity and water. Aside from that, she treats everyone in her team as a family and helps them complete their own visions. Ragne is well respected in the community because she keeps her word in everything, she says she will get done. She is not only a visionary but also an action taker. She will not stop until a project is well organized, executed, and delivered. Over the past year, Ragne has continued to grow the World Women Conference and Awards and bring in the right leaders to assist her in this project. You can simply know her character by simply asking her what WWCA is for her, and she will tell you WWCA is everyone's organization, not just hers. She is a great team player who empowers others to do their best because she is the perfect example.

Testimonial By Cristal Balk, WWCA Global Marketing Leader

Vision Statement: To celebrate innovative and extraordinary women and create a global community of women that is an active social, economic, and cultural force in the development of nations.

During World War II, Winston Churchill said:

Greeks don't fight like heroes,

Heroes fight like Greeks.

Ragne uses the same analogy and says:

Ragne does not act like a Visionary Woman,

Visionary Women want to act like Ragne.

And here is why:

- She has a clear, realistic, and great vision for the World
- She wants to improve the lives of deprived women and children
- She is inspiring, engaging, and collaborative
- She promotes participation and empowerment
- She involves and supports others in achieving their dreams
- She has a Resolute and Unwavering character
- She is Self-Motivated with an exemplary Positive Self-Esteem
- She is also a Purposeful and Visionary Leader driven by Quality and Ethics
- Charismatic in her approach and Magnetic with her talk
- Enthusiastically encourages and builds confidence, trust, and self-reliance
- But most importantly, she autographs her work with EXCELLENCE all the time.

Testimonial By Dr. John N Kalaras, Professor at DeVry and Keller Graduate School of Management in Chicago IL. USA, for 42 years. He served on **The President's Business Advisory Council** in 2005 through 2009 under President

George W. Bush, responsible for Educational and Training. In 1999 UNESCO recognized Dr. Kalaras as "The Professor of The Year."

Quote

"I have learned that people will forget what you said, people will forget what you did, but people will never forget how you made them feel."

Maya Angelou

Admiration of a Visionary Leader

The late Princess deeply inspires Ragne; what makes her so timeless is her "sense of style and purpose," how she was "independent… thoughtful and modern about her approach to things" and "always the one to set the trends rather than follow them."

We all can relate to Grace Kelly's fashion, style, and philanthropy that has caught the attention and has fascinated the world for decades. Ragne admires her for her passion for empowerment, equal rights, and desire to create a better world.

Grace Kelly dedicated herself to charity and cultural work, and this is where Ragne also sees her life's purpose. Ragne aims to reposition women for high performance, improved leadership, and strong participation in society's economic and social development. As a visionary, she celebrates innovative and extraordinary women creating a global community of women active in social, economic, and cultural forces in developing nations. Every girl and woman deserve the opportunity to have her own voice and to have human rights.

Journey of Discovering the Greatness Within

Being born in a previous Soviet Union country is a challenge in itself. She had to learn how to strive in a very competitive world and struggle with the lack of support and mentorship. She had to learn the hard way and often asked what it means to be empowered? To empower through education is her life purpose and the main reason why she leads women worldwide. To be empowered is to authentically step into who we are as women, embrace the feminine, and question the very masculine world we have helped create. We need to take 100% responsibility for what is happening in our society instead of waiting for someone else to fix it and commit to educating and inspiring future generations differently.

To do that, we must first look at ourselves and understand what it means to be authentic. Who are we really underneath all of the doubts, fears, and insecurities? Who do we want to be, and what energy do we want to take out into the world?

This truth will impact and change our ecosystems because having the courage to bring our whole selves into our leadership has the power to change the world. The untapped potential of women worldwide in every walk of life is a priority that requires our urgent attention. The fact is, women still bear the biggest burden of poverty, and most people living in poverty are women. We know why and how excluding women impacts societies and economies. By World Women Empowerment and others, much is being done to advance women's well-being and expand their roles as political, economic, family, and social leaders. But to make gender equality happen, a concerted focus on legal reform and ending violence against women is needed. Though this is happening, more needs to be done quickly to benefit all, women and men, girls, and boys.

According to Ragne's definition: "A hero is someone who has given his or her life to something bigger than oneself." Anyone can become a hero—on purpose or even accidentally. But it involves a painful evolution that is a prerequisite to greatness. It all begins with a call to adventure, a challenge or quest that presents itself to an ordinary person in the ordinary world. Initially, the person is afraid and refuses that call. Like Ragne was. But with guidance from a mentor, she overcame her fears, crossed the threshold, and committed to the journey. So can you.

Along the way, we are tested, meet allies and enemies, and prepare for an ordeal—some kind of showdown or difficulty that will truly test our mettle. The ordeal forces us to face our worst fears. And when we survive this, the ordinary person is a hero and is rewarded, usually with knowledge or insight.

So, what did Ragne have to do in order to get where she is? She had to slay her dragons. And the formula she used is not just a way to interpret the great tales of historical and contemporary myths. It also lends meaning to our everyday existence, putting our individual struggles in a noble context. The trials and tribulations we face and survive may not seem heroic. But knowing that we grow as a result of them and that this can make us into better people makes it easier to be brave.

The reward is not the end of the story, however. Next, the hero must return to the ordinary world where the journey began, transformed by their experience. Finally, the reborn hero in ourselves shares what we have learned on the journey with others.

Empowering Results

Women's empowerment has five components:

1. Women's sense of self-worth
2. Their right to have and to determine choices
3. Their right to have access to opportunities and resources
4. Their right to have the power to control their own lives, both within and outside the home
5. Their ability to influence the direction of social change, creating a more just social and economic order, nationally and internationally.

In this context, essential tools for empowering women and girls to claim their rights include: education, training, awareness-raising, building self-confidence, expansion of choices, increased access to and control over resources, and transforming the structures and institutions that reinforce perpetuate gender discrimination and inequality. This is what the family of Female leaders at the World Women Conference & Awards does. Ragne is humbled to be the founder of that organization.

Ragne's passion is to help women, and her energy is the beat of her heart and soul in every action she sets forth. She is a proud member of Ancestral Nations A.C. Cannativo movement of indigenous hands, with this movement, they are developing sustainable ecosystems within the indigenous communities of Mexico, hand in hand with the native tribes of Baja California Sur.

Today, Ragne builds global partnerships with the vision of establishing local chapters in Estonia, the USA, and Mexico that promote and accomplish gender equality and empowerment.

And finally, her legacy to this world is the Untold Story Foundation (USF). It is a global family of women in Action for A BETTER SOCIETY! They are a social service-oriented organization whose mission is to bring together women leaders to provide humanitarian service and advance goodwill and peace around the world. USF will serve as a resource and a voice for its community. They are seeking to improve the lives of women and girls worldwide. The USF focuses on education. Specifically, in educating on the environment, health, hunger, malnutrition, and human rights advocating for the rights of women and girls worldwide and contributing to the global community through its Chapters and Online community, which will constantly provide development funds education awards.

When caring women join together, roll up their sleeves and take action to make their community better, it's the most beautiful thing to happen to society—and a fulfilling moment for every woman involved. That's society's heart cry that women will arise and take up their roles as Incubators of Life and release life into the world. Being a woman is about playing the mother role across all spheres of society, leading by example, building relationships, and improving the world through love and giving.

'Our mission is to raise a global family of over 1 billion caring women serving together to make a lasting impact and change more lives in their community.'

Join us if you want to impact and add value to our global network of women whose objectives are: Raising the status of women through education, raising awareness, literacy, training, and equipping, and allowing women to make life-determining decisions in their daily life and through the different problems in society. Build awareness of business innovations that accelerate women's empowerment and have a real impact on the quality of life for women, men, families, and communities. Identify key actions to address the financing gap for women's empowerment. Drive change and commit to scaled-up partnerships for women's economic empowerment. Provide women with the educational tools to have greater responsibility to take care of their needs and their family. To sponsor, host and/or participate in events and activities that promote women empowerment education and training. We are looking for untold stories and hidden heroes. Are you one of them?

The Importance of Women's Contributions

Our passion is to empower through education, creating access for opportunities through the innovative global network serving women from all walks of life while positively impacting the community. The WWCA provides the World's women an ecosystem. An opportunity to empower, network, and create change for a positive force for good in the verticals of health, education, personal development, and wealth creation. The WWCA is proactive in cultural development within and between nations, without bias or conditions, and allows interaction with an international audience through the organization. Our Global networking platform creates access for opportunities to connect, network, share, learn & invest in your personal growth. WWCA brings top online experts in the world to give you the techniques, secrets, and strategies that are working RIGHT NOW to grow your business, including virtual presence. Connect with Like-Minded People & Partner with Like-Valued People. DO YOU WANT TO MAKE A DIFFERENCE BY DOING SOMETHING THAT MAKES A DIFFERENCE WITH PEOPLE WHO MAKE A DIFFERENCE AT A TIME THAT MAKES A DIFFERENCE? This is what WWCA Family is all about!

Action is what converts human dreams into significance. Seizing significant opportunities like WWCA membership with collaboration with StarpreneursTV will leverage visibility, exposure, credibility, and innovation. You disrupt the way you are doing your business and communicate with your audience. As a brand, you can harness the power of this new digital channel. In addition to building your authority, you can now reach millions of targeted audiences around the world while tapping into a billion-dollar market.

We are giving the voice to untold stories and empowering through education. We search for untold stories at Dominate the Decade with Ragne Sinikas talk show. We provide the voice and amplify the impact of fascinating leaders who dare to be different and be more of themselves. We value diversity and inclusion. Leadership truly starts within. Ragne believes that pursuing your dreams with powerful intentions and a sense of purpose requires a call from within yourself to activate that desire. The power of presence ignites your capacity to create a remarkable future by transforming that intention into future action. We are on a mission to find hidden heroes with untold stories. Those stories have the power to change our ecosystems. Are you one of them? Let's discover your voice and share your message. The road to success will be unique, but everyone must overcome certain common themes to reach their personal or business potential. So the Dominate the Decade with Ragne Sinikas is a talk show where she asks the entrepreneurial rock stars to lend some insights into their secret sauce for success and their three recommendations How to Dominate the Decade. Think of this advice as the defining moment that can potentially change the audience's life. If you feel that you are aligned and want to be part of this platform, please schedule the time for the interview.

Greatest Achievement

Ragne's acute awareness throughout the years has provided her with the ability to contribute with her heart and soul to helping everyone she meets. Ragne's insight into working in many countries has built bridges of communication, strengthening initiatives between women and local and state governments. Ragne was born into a country under the control of the Soviet Union, where there were no civil rights. The impact of her childhood has set a solid foundation on her quest for women's empowerment in education, health, and civil rights.

Her courage is always present in every step of her life, always building teams of loyal women that champion and help the less fortunate girls and women. Ragne's strength and inspiration are powered by the energy and accomplishment of every woman she helps.

Ragne's commitment to achieving empowerment through education is key to obtaining gender equality. Ragne's involvement with university students in Mexico has inspired many to participate in multiplying the gender equality movement. Ragne works with kids who have health challenges such as the need for heart surgeries. With over 100 surgeries in the last 24 months, she has changed the lives of 100 families. One hundred women who lost hope now have a healthy kid with a strong heart and an amazing future. Ragne's passion is helping Women. Ragne's energy is the beat of her heart and soul in every action she sets forth. Today, Ragne builds global partnerships with the vision of establishing local chapters in Estonia, the USA, and Mexico that promote and accomplish gender equality and empowerment.

An Inclusive and Diverse World

Leveraging technology for good and delivering impact is a rising trend. Using AI-powered solutions for business transformation and advancing diversity and inclusion in the workplace is an interesting trend. Ragne came across a company, Predixa D&I, https://www.predixa.ai/. They support organizations to assess where a company is with its Diversity and Inclusion journey providing D&I and HR leaders with data and analytics linked to business and an action plan with priorities they can address. This changes the dynamic to one that is data and insights-driven, empowering leaders with the right metrics to move forward with concrete actions, delivering progress on diversity and inclusion and other business issues.

1. The world of work continues to challenge our perceptions of power. Organizations become increasingly aware of the benefits of diversity and inclusion to keep pace with innovation and business opportunities; the need for a new type of leadership – one with humanity at its core – has never been more apparent.

'Leadership is less about the position you hold than the influence you have. It's about doing world-class work, playing at your peak, and leaving people better than you found them. It's about Leading Without a Title. '- Robin Sharma

2. An Equal Society. When we go back to our humanity, we leave gender behind. We leave stereotypes behind. We leave limitations behind. Instead, we focus on leveraging our uniqueness, working with both our masculine and feminine aspects to find a complementary balance between two forces that together make us human. The leaders of tomorrow are those who can explore the full range of their masculine and feminine, enabling them to express their life-force energy consciously. They come from a place of authenticity where vulnerability is a strength and labels are only found on the back of our clothing. While we cannot flip these judgments overnight, we can all do the inner work required to develop greater empathy and sensitivity toward others and lead from a place of clarity, always showing up as our whole selves.

We live in a time when whole industries, economies, and political landscapes are becoming more and more volatile and uncertain. Businesses with leaders who know how to connect to the center of their inner being and lead from a place of "knowing" will adapt more easily and thus be the most successful.

3. Finding the balance. Paving the way for an equal society means that businesses must embrace difference and take action against all forms of dominance (bullying, sexual harassment, inflated egos). Society sees firefighters as males and nurses as females. Male entrepreneurs stand for ego, resilience, and over-confidence; female entrepreneurs denote service and the tendency to be risk-averse. Men are steady, and women are emotional – we tend to accept, rather than question, the status quo of this belief system. These stereotypes are real, and these antiquated attitudes of "men's work" versus "women's work" continue to hold considerable influence when it comes to business decisions. Prejudices are rife, from candidate placements to salaries, incentives, and performance evaluations. They stem from outdated patriarchal systems and how we have learned to see ourselves in relation to others. So, where does change start then?

4. "Companies need open and explicit discussion of how differences can be used as sources of individual and organizational effectiveness."

Strategies to Succeed in Our COVID Changed World

Ragne is proud to market a brand-new digital TV channel called Starpreneurs TV. At Starpreneurs TV, we showcase world-class influencers, industry experts, and those who have a powerful message by having their own custom-branded TV shows or mini-series on Roku and Amazon Fire TV. Her goal is to help individuals and businesses reach millions of people around the world, tap into a multi-billion-dollar market, add new income streams to their business portfolios, be on the cutting edge of technology, and take advantage of a brand-new digital channel through the power of TV.

Author's Quote

Pursuing your dreams with a powerful intention and a sense of purpose requires a call from within yourself to activate that desire. The power of presence ignites your capacity to create a remarkable future by transforming that intention into future action. Ragne Sinikas

Bio

Mrs. Ragne Sinikas is a social entrepreneur, philanthropist, online marketer, founder of World Women Empowerment, Starpreneurs TV. Real Estate Developer, an international speaker, coach of the Change Makers, global award winner with her Dominate the Decade Podcast. She has over 15 years of sales leadership in developing and implementing sales and business plans internationally, in several industry sectors. She is focused on women's empowerment through education, skills-building, and entrepreneurial programs that create new opportunities for women to sustain their livelihoods. Ragne's vision is to strengthen and preserve cultural and community development and to build key relationships with different organizations and potential partners within the international community.

Ragne Sinikas is a seasoned entrepreneur. The Founder of World Women Conference & Awards, Real Estate Developer & Investor, Starpreneurs TV, Complex Holding, Untold Story Foundation, Change Makers Coach, Public Speaker, Philanthropist.

Country Estonia

Learn more about this author

https://allmylinks.com/ragne-sinikas

Chapter 2

Permission to Succeed

Forbes Riley
The Queen of Pitch

Introduction

Forbes Riley had a career as an actress and a television host in Los Angeles. One day she walked into a studio, and they said, 'sell me this pen.' She had a bad reaction as she didn't like the concept of selling. Her natural response to this request was far from a typical sales pitch. The words she used drew the listener into a story, connecting to the audience.

Her natural flowing words were a hit, and this launched her career to become the $2.5 billion dollar Queen of Pitch.

Forbes bought too many clothes from salesgirls who said that the clothes looked good on her. When she got home and tried them on again, they did not look great, so they are now in the back of her closet. That is the experience many people have when they are sold something.

Pitching originated on the boardwalks of Atlantic City with guys talking about amazing knives and kitchen gadgets, but that's not her path. Forbes is one of the only women in a sea of pitchmen. She instinctively understands features and benefits and how to get somebody's credit card out of their pocket to buy what you have. She has now taken and mastered the concept of how to pitch and taught 1000s of students how to stop selling and start exciting, engaging, and enrolling people into your world.

Forbes explains and leads you through a process that draws your ideal client to you where they want more of what you have to offer. She does this in a fun way! What she does is ideal for network marketers, small businesses, and entrepreneurs because you don't have a company or a business without sales, and you certainly don't have a profit.

Her career has grossed over $2.5 billion dollars in product sales and led to a lifestyle that she could only have dreamed of. As an awkward, ugly little girl growing up on Long Island, New York. Forbes Riley invites you to uncover your true potential and stop playing small if you've got a big idea. The world needs to know it, and she is here to help you master the art of the pitch. The world is your oyster.

Mission

As a high-level Pitch and Sales Coach, Forbes's specialty is crafting your verbal pitch. From how you introduce yourself, position your product, service idea, and close.

She invites you to figure out what your public persona is and what your business is? How do you make money? How do you generate contacts? How do you generate leads?

Her thought is that if you make your stories matter to other people's ears, they will want to engage with you and seek to connect with you.

Her mission over the years has evolved as everyone would expect it to. She has made an amazing living; she raised two beautiful kids as a single mom. And now, she is focused on entrepreneurs, dreamers, coaches, and network marketers. Helping them understand that once they master the art of the pitch, they can live a powerful and very empowered life. Anywhere, anytime.

Mission Statement: To inspire people to dream big, empower them to live their best life, and ignite a fire that motivates them to implement positive habits and take massive action steps!

Vision

Forbes has a philosophy that she teaches; stop talking and start communicating!

But how does a person achieve clarity in their communications? Forbes has a solution. And it starts with knowing what you want. Knowing what your business is, who it benefits and how to get your message out to the world. She offers exceptional courses to assist you in becoming a media master. Once you have your pitch and media message nailed, she will take you on a journey to discover and articulate your persona, which opens up your world of public media options.

Vision Statement: To live in a world where leaders have integrity, conviction, passion, and of course, a vision that, through clear communication, whether verbal or written, they will inspire others to take action.

Quote

"Our deepest fear is not that we are inadequate. Our deepest fear is that we are powerful beyond measure. It is our light, not our darkness, that most frightens us. We ask ourselves, who am I to be brilliant, gorgeous, talented, fabulous? Actually, who are you not to be? You are a child of God. You're playing small does not serve the world. There is nothing enlightened about shrinking so that other people won't feel insecure around you. We are all meant to shine, as children do. We were born to make manifest the glory of God that is within us. It is not just in some of us; it is in everyone. And as we let our own light shine, we unconsciously give other people permission to do the same. As we are liberated from our own fear, our presence automatically liberates others."

Marianne Williamson

Admiration of a Visionary Leader

A visionary female leader that Forbes Riley views as a role model is Marianne Williamson. She has always tied in her spiritual, political, and philosophical views. And it just made sense. She's quoted saying it is not our darkness that most frightens us but our light. We were all meant to shine. It's not just in some of us; it's in all of us. And when we step up and shine, we give permission for others to do the same.

Journey of Discovering the Greatness Within

In Forbes' youth, she spent a lot of time with her father. He was an inventor, a magician, and worked for a printing company. She loved to spend time with her dad as he opened her eyes to what was possible.

She loved to make her mom and dad smile. A family highlight was to watch the Oscars. This is likely where Forbes first formed the desire to be an actress. Forbes was an inspired little girl and very different from the kids she grew up with. Her head was swirling with imagination and thinking anything was possible. She felt she could do anything she wanted and has lived most of her life with a mindset that she has permission to do just that - anything. At times, this seemed to go against the rules, but it gave her a sense of control deep inside. Control over her life and what she wanted.

Forbes's life has been riddled with trauma. Her mother was held at gunpoint while thieves stole all the household valuables. Her father had an accident with a printing press that hospitalized him for almost two years. This accident changed the family forever. Forbes learned that there would no longer be the money for her to get a higher education. She was devastated by her father's injury, and now this. Her mother came up with the idea that her bright daughter should enter a contest, a contest that is based on a young women's mental abilities and not just her looks. As Forbes and her mom discussed this in the hospital, a plastic surgeon overheard the conversation. A short time later, her crooked nose was straightened, and she confidently entered the contest and won.

This led to a directional change in her life. But all was not rosy. Forbes has witnessed atrocities from a young man who was like a son to her being shot down on the street and left to die being witness to the mass shootings in Las Vegas. These events interfered with her clear thinking, and PTSD (post-traumatic stress disorder) became a part of her life. Her self-care had diminished to a critical point. If she had gotten on a specific plane (one involved in the 9-11 terrors), she wouldn't be with us today. She didn't get on that plane because she was critically dehydrated. She was rescued and recovered to be with us today.

Forbes wanted to discover what made some people great leaders. Why some are wealthy and successful, while others seem to stumble without success, her personal journey led her to an answer. Successful people all continue to learn.

Forbes Riley, a mother of twins, has vast life experiences. She has worked on Broadway, movies, TV, superstar infomercial host, and many other areas. She has reinvented herself several times but has always focused on learning and achieving. Her acting and improv skills combined with a passion for storytelling have led her on a path to become a motivational speaker, role model, and CEO of a business training institute. She believes her training institute has positively impacted the lives of thousands, far beyond the impact that a movie or television show would ever have.

We should learn and note life's lessons with each life event. Here are a few things that can help you move beyond the difficult times and help you find what it is you desire.

> Believe in yourself.
> Decide what you want.
> Live with permission.
> Continue to learn.
> Find a good coach.

Empowering Results

Women are, by nature, nurturers. We are mothers. We give life; we actually birth it. And it puts women in a very unique perspective. Forbes can remember when she was pregnant with her twins, thinking how horrific war was. How horrible to send your sons and daughters off to fight. While she admires patriots, men, and women who serve, she thinks it's a great sacrifice for the mother who gave birth to that soldier who puts his life on the line for our country. Forbes has spent a lot of time coming to understand what it means to be a woman in a man's world. Maybe just a woman in the world. We are not as physically strong as men. We do not run races as fast as men. But if you take out the physical difference and add in computers and AI, men and women are on an equal playing field. Women see problems, initiatives, friendships, and community differently than men do simply by the nature of how we are designed.

Forbes cares for students, which is often shown when she devotes her time to her classes. She calls an Ace an Ace, so you know it is from a place of truth when she speaks to you.

Her students respect her. The training provided has improved their lives. Her community is second to none, with enormous support and caring for each other. That comes from the leadership. Step into her world, and you can feel the high vibrational energy that lifts each community member.

The Importance of Women's Contributions

To dream means closing your eyes and creating visions of a life you want. As the story goes, imagine JK Rowling was homeless sitting on a train with a pen and some napkins when she created the entire Harry Potter series. This woman became a billionaire. She had her kids and no money to pay for dinner. But her vision could really bring her up in the world, and she chose never to give up. Another young woman named Sara Blakely had a goofy complaint that her undergarments designed to hold you in caused horrible lines. What if you could make stretchy support hose that had no lines and maybe stockings that have no feet so you could wear them when you're wearing sandals? She was put down a lot and told that this would never work. And today, she sits at the top of a billion-dollar company called Spanx. Forbes has listened to her speak about how it was one person - one vision. When she launched in department stores, she would stand in the stores, take customer surveys and help propel the brand. Not sure if she realized her vision would propel her to become a billionaire. Oprah Winfrey was a young woman in a time when race was an issue. She was raised in a very poor environment, molested, hurt, told that she didn't matter. But somewhere inside of her, she had a vision that she did. Today, we know her because of a national talk show she created; she became a billionaire because she would not give up or give in. Being a woman in today's world is exciting. Perhaps different than it's ever been. And sometimes, just as challenging as it's always been, she has hit her head against the wall many times as a young actress who was chased around the office desk or asked to lunch with an agent or producer. These meetings were not intended to be in a restaurant at a hotel but actually in their hotel room. This is long before the "Me Too" movement was the thing. Forbes is so glad that she has lived to see young actresses, models, and just women stand up against the powerful men they've had to face. Whether it was a Harvey Weinstein in the movie industry, or the sex trafficking trade with Jeffrey Epstein, all of a sudden, it's come to light that there have been crimes against humanity because we were women.

Welcome, 2022. Forbes puts forth the thought that the only way that change continues to stay constant is if we remain diligent. There are those in the world who would take a woman's rights away for what she can do with her body. I'm not saying whether abortion is right or wrong. That is a moral choice that I believe each woman gets to make for herself. But she has a very hard time understanding a world where someone else tells you the kind of control you have over your body. Or the kind of world that demands that children are born into a world where there's no mother or father to love them. They would face growing up abandoned, hurt, trafficked, or killed. She has seen that happen.

A way to support women is to offer them an ear to listen and help them build their confidence to bring their vision and their voice to the world.

Greatest Achievement

Having her twins later in life is her greatest achievement. Being a mother has been rewarding; although challenging, she wouldn't change a thing. She is proud of her children and blessed to have them both involved in her business.

An Inclusive and Diverse World

The world needs to accept diversification; it is how things change and improve. By accepting everyone, we open up a world of possibilities. When people are accepted and included, they become increasingly open and share unique ideas from the heart.

Forbes Riley's students are from every background and every nation. No matter your skin color, accent, or whether you are rich, poor, abused, or blessed, everyone is welcome in her community. When you are a part of her community, you are always welcome, and you can find support on most anything you may need.

> Respect others.
> Be authentic.
> Help others to succeed.
> Believe in yourself.
> Listen to understand.

Strategies To Succeed in Our COVID Changed World

Before COVID struck the world, Forbes had accumulated a wealth of knowledge which she shared at in-person events. She was already well versed in teaching and leading people to be better versions of themselves and methods to excellence in their business.

She knew the power of the internet and took the time to study the power of social media and systems to perfect time management on the internet. In 2020 she stepped up to help others. She launched a new company starting with her pitch masterclass training created with her 18-year-old daughter Makenna. This class offers people a way to communicate with clarity creating interest in what you are saying. She then took her experience and skills of excellence in front of a camera; she delivered them to students through Zoom classes to reach a worldwide audience. Forbes is an unstoppable force as she continues these pieces of training to develop her students further in presenting themselves on other people's platforms. This course, known as OPP, has skyrocketed many students to be in the public's eye with an aura of confidence.

Some other courses and events have been launched during COVID that have been a blessing to her students in new understandings, knowledge, confidence, and community. She invites you to experience her Sunday evening Pitch Masterclass and look at how she can change your communication style and improve your communication outcomes.

In 2020 there was a new and exciting app launched called Clubhouse. It was social media in a new form. It is an audio-only app where people come together worldwide to discuss and learn from a vast array of professionals and various topics.

We all had been isolated from face-to-face encounters for most of 2020, and we needed to regain the human need of being social. Forbes joined Clubhouse in January 2021. It was a lifesaver, a platform where people could once again hang out and talk to each other in groups. She hadn't realized how starved she was for communication and connecting with long-lost friendships. You can make new friends on social media and create meaningful business relationships.

Forbes didn't sit back and wait to see what would happen during these years; she stepped up and helped the world.

Author's quote

Dream it - Believe it - Achieve it

Bio

Forbes Riley is known as the $2.5 Billion Dollar Queen of Pitch. An Award-Winning TV Host, Author, Motivational Speaker, Entrepreneur, and one of the World's Leading Health & Wellness experts (National Fitness Hall of Fame inductee). She has hosted 192 infomercials and appeared on HSN and QVC worldwide, promoting healthy lifestyle and fitness products. Through online and virtual training, she teaches people to pitch their products, service, or business so they can easily and effectively get their ideas out to the world.

She was voted as one of the "Top 20 Most inspiring People on Television" through her roles as a spokesperson, broadcast journalist, and Success/Results Coach to celebrities, sales teams, and CEOs. She is touring the globe and sharing at Colleges, Sales Meetings, and from Boardrooms to Global Skypes. She is a dynamic Motivational Speaker and role model for the Success of Women in Business, Sales Training, and Leadership Coaching. As a motivational keynote speaker - she's affectionately called "The Female Tony Robbins."

Learn more about this author

Instagram: instagram.com/forbes_riley

YouTube: youtube.com/forbesriley

Facebook: facebook.com/forbesriley

Twitter: twitter.com/forbesriley

Website: www.forbesriley.com

Clubhouse: @forbersriley

Link: www.forbesriley.tv

Chapter 3

Your Inner Wisdom - Activate Your Caring Magic

Francesca Richardson, PhD.

The Inner Wisdom Psychotherapist

Introduction

Dr. Francesca Richardson is known as the Inner Wisdom Psychotherapist because – as a psychoanalyst and hypnotherapist for over 30 years, she has helped people heal issues stored deep within them so they can learn to love themselves. One major way she works is to help people recognize the Magic of their Caring abilities, their ability to change other people's reality through caring. She calls this their 'Caring Magic' and helps them recognize their need for self-care to replenish their caring abilities.

She also helps people to transform their inner critic. The inner critic tells them they are not doing things right or are not doing enough. Once the inner critic is transformed, they can treat themselves in a sacred way, recognizing their innate value on this earth. This helps them shine their light and best use their Caring Magic to achieve peace, emotional freedom, and personal success.

Mission

Dr. Francesca Richardson has been a mental health professional and educator for over 30 years. She integrates processes for healing emotional problems such as PTSD. The processes she uses include psychoanalysis, hypnotherapy, and EMDR. Francesca also teaches and trains others in these methods. She is a Nature Sacred Fellow for The Nova Institute for Health of People, Places, and Planet, focusing on researching nature and well-being.

Mission Statement: To help people heal from traumas, care for themselves, and learn to act and communicate with compassion.

Vision

Trauma comes in many forms. Sometimes a person's empathy and giving qualities (Caring Magic) are not honored, boundaries are not respected, and they are not treated in a sacred way. Through Francesca's experience, she has seen that people need guidance to heal their past traumas. Once the healing occurs, they can develop compassion for themselves and others. These improvements lead to better communication. They can then choose to create a life in alignment with their soul's purpose, which helps improve life for all on the planet.

Self-care is not selfish. Refuel your Caring Magic through caring for yourself.

Vision Statement: To live in a world where all people have healed from past trauma, caring for themselves and others with compassion.

Once people heal their past traumas, recognize themselves as Sacred beings, and recognize the Magic of their Caring abilities, they increase compassion for themselves and others. They can then create a life in alignment with their soul's purpose.

Quote of a Visionary Leader.

"While men represent powerful activity as assertion and aggression, women, in contrast, portray acts of nurturance as acts of strength." Carol Gilligan

Admiration of a Visionary Leader

Carol Gilligan is an American feminist, ethicist, researcher, and psychologist best known for her work on ethical community and ethical relationships. She is the originator of the ethic of care. This philosophical perspective suggests that women tend to value self-sacrifice as the highest good. But Dr. Gilligan points out that what is best for women is self-care balanced with care for others. Dr. Richardson is also a feminist, researcher, and psychotherapist, learning along with her clients to achieve that balance.

Four concrete steps:

1. Identify what gets in the way of you recognizing your Inner Wisdom.
2. Identify what depletes your Caring Magic, your ability to change reality through caring.
3. Heal traumas getting in the way of your Sacred Self and Caring Magic.
4. Bring the power of your Inner Wisdom and your Caring Magic out into the world.

Journey of Discovering the Greatness Within

Despite addictions and mental and physical illnesses in her family, Dr. Richardson went on to become a psychotherapist. At age 50, despite a learning disability and poor math skills, she studied math to improve her GRE score, and based on that score, she got a full scholarship for her PhD. Since then, she has been helping people take charge of their lives and break free from traumas, emotional problems, and limiting beliefs.

Empowering Results

Dr. Francesca Richardson is like most women; she has nurtured and guided others most of her life. She works with individuals and in group sessions at her private practice. Dr. Richardson has guided students at the bachelor's and master's levels through her classes and provides supervision and consultation to new psychotherapists and hypnotherapists. Supporting and nurturing is not just part of her profession, but it is deep-rooted in her persona. Dr. Richardson has been involved in church activities, guiding and nurturing people within the congregation. She co-led a program to run lay-led covenant group circles and wrote the exercises and activities for the groups to follow.

Thousands of women of all ages have been helped in her psychotherapy practice for over 30 years. Francesca is there to help them feel empowered to make changes they need to make, to be assertive, and shine their light in the world. She helps young women sort out their future life, career paths and negotiate relationships. During mid-life and older ages, women are helped with the changes, losses, and search for meaning inherent at each stage.

The world has not yet fully recognized the value of women's caring work, making it difficult for women to value themselves and their contributions to the world. One of the ways women give care is through 'emotion work' (Hochschild, 1979) which is the management of others' emotions. Women listen, validate, encourage, intuit feelings, provide support, help people feel better, or see a new perspective. They are encouraged to do this in families and businesses. This activity is called emotion work.

Women's perspectives are important due to their natural tendency to be nurturing and compassionate. These tendencies are due to higher estrogen levels and socialization towards caring rather than competing. All women need to step out of their comfort zone and starting practicing self-care.

Here I am with my other Avatar, Diana Rigg's Emma Peel from the British Avengers.

Dr. Francesca Richardson believes women need to learn self-care as they often self-sacrifice too much. Women tend to think in terms of caring for others and are encouraged to consider others' needs over their own. This tendency is part of the theory of the Ethic of Care. The researcher Carol Gilligan noted this tendency as part of women's moral development when she noticed that women make moral decisions differently than men (1981). Her research showed that women tend to value self-sacrifice more than self-care. Much in society shows us that women who self-sacrifice are considered morally and spiritually superior to those who practice self-care. This type of thinking can especially affect work situations where women are not remunerated for the time and value of their work.

Dr. Francesca Richardson has helped thousands of people to heal emotionally and spiritually throughout her career. Hundreds of people have been trained and benefited from the bachelor and master levels to clinicians at colleges and institutions in the realm of social work, psychology, psychoanalysis, transpersonal hypnotherapy, and EMDR.

Francesca has completed research and spoken on the topic of female family caregivers of dementia patients. In her practice with clients and within her research, she found that many people, especially those nurturing and caring for others, believe that self-care is selfish. They have difficulty balancing their self-care with caring for others. Dr. Richardson researched and presented Caring Magic, archetypes, relationships, healing the inner critic, and ecopsychology.

Greatest Achievement

Dr. Francesca Richardson has been guiding, assisting, and helping to heal thousands of people emotionally and spiritually. She has educated hundreds of students in the last 30 years.

Dr. Francesca was 1 out of 100 of our best-selling authors from the 1 Habit book series who was asked to envision what that World will look like and what Habits people can instill in themselves to not only survive but to thrive like never before.

An Inclusive and Diverse World

Practically all ancient cultures practice deep inner work. Dr. Francesca Richardson has been helping many individuals from different cultures, spiritual beliefs, gender identifications, and relationship orientations. She works with them to heal from traumas using practices for inner work. The people she has helps seek self-transformation to reach self-awareness and self-love. The inner work fosters and encourages discovering new perspectives and beliefs that serve the individual to achieve success and seek a sense of belonging. People practicing inner work do it for five main reasons listed below:

1) People need guidance to become compassionate and forgiving and manage their Caring Magic in healthy ways.
2) People need a sense of hope.
3) People need education on the importance of diversity and inclusion and how it can benefit all.
4) People need to process their fear of difference and loss of resources.
5) People need guidance to learn how to implement their new ways of thinking and behaving.

Doing our inner work helps make our outer work easier to achieve because as we change our perspective, we create new decisions and access new resources leading to new actions.

Strategies to Succeed in Our COVID Changed World

In 2020 when the pandemic quarantine hit, she could not see clients in her office. To continue helping people, she needed new skills and technical knowledge. With her determination, she studied and learned what was needed, then transferred her private practice and teaching of hypnotherapy entirely online. She began running online group therapy sessions, engaged in live podcasts and speaks on the Clubhouse platform to start conversations on emotional and spiritual healing for people around the world. She found that having focus and determination was essential for success.

Author's Quote

"Self-care is not selfish. Refuel your Caring Magic through caring for yourself." Dr. Francesca Richardson

Bio

Francesca Richardson, MSW, PhD

Dr. Richardson is a psychoanalyst, trauma therapist and EMDR practitioner, transpersonal hypnotherapist, educator, hypnotherapy trainer, and researcher. Her research focuses on women's development, spirituality, and the ecopsychological connection of nature and well-being. For over 30 years, she has helped people individually and in group settings to release problematic personal patterns so they can align with their soul's purpose.

Hamilton College - BA

New York University - MSW

Catholic University - PhD

Post-graduate training:

Psychoanalytic Training, Training Institute for Mental Health, Certificate 1995

Training in Supervision of the Psychoanalytic Process for Supervision of Psychoanalytic Candidates, Contemporary Center for Advanced Psychoanalytic Studies 1997-1999

ASCH Hypnotherapy Training -- 1999

Wellness Institute Hypnotherapy Training - 2001

EMDR Training 1&2, with Laurie Parnell -- 2002

Carol Lampman - Integral Breathwork Training 1 & 2 - 2004

Accelerated Resolution Therapy, Master Level -- 2019

Selected Papers:

· Caregiving as Ministry: Perceptions of African American Caregivers of Elders. Families in Society · Jan 1, 2014. Families in Society · Jan 1, 2014

· The clarity process: Using heart-centered regression techniques in couple therapy -- An object relations and systems theory approach. The clarity process: Using heart-centered regression techniques in couple therapy -- An object relations and systems theory approach. Journal of Heart-Centered Therapies · Jan 1, 2008.

Selected Presentations:

· A Cry in the Wilder city: A Qualitative Analysis of Nature's Effects on Wellbeing as Expressed in Urban Park Bench Journal Entries. Poster Presented at the ICIMH Conference, Phoenix, Arizona, 2020.

· Pathways to Well-Being through Bench Journal Entries at Urban Parks:

A Qualitative Study. Presentation at the Nature and Health Conference, Seattle, WA, 2021

Contact me through my website:

www.innerpotential.com

Or my facebook page:

https://www.facebook.com/FrancescaRichardsonPhD

Chapter 4

The Power of Awakening Your Inner Warrior

Diane Lang

Akashic Record Consultant, Intuitive Channel

Introduction

Diane knew that she was different at a very young age. She started out life in a small town in Saskatchewan, Canada. She recognized early in life she had a unique gift for imparting wisdom to people of all ages. She also called out hypocrisy, stood up to bullies, and did not back down regardless of their age or size.

She took that strength and harnessed it into helping others awaken their inner warrior, set healthy boundaries, and recognize that we are all the captains at the helm of our own ship.

Mission

Diane's studies led her to acquire a deep understanding of many energy healing modalities and an understanding of universal laws. After several personal health issues, Diane wanted to know more about her soul's story, which led her to become a Certified Akashic Record Consultant. Diane uses her natural intuitive gifts to help her clients discover what conscious and unconscious blocks hinder their success in any given area of their lives. This leads her clients to a new level of empowerment, creating the life they truly desire.

Mission Statement

Diane's mission is to help people understand and balance the harmonic energies between their human experience and their spiritual story to align and draw a more empowered, purpose-filled life to themselves.

Vision

Diane specializes in helping people overcome adversity and struggles to rise above life's painful experiences. Whereby they no longer settle for crumbs or sit at the back of the bus in their own life story. None of us signed up to spend our lives at the back of the bus! Diane loves all things spiritual in nature and thrives on seeing her clients tap into their inherent gifts and use them to bring joy and abundance into their lives.

Vision Statement

Diane's vision is to see the world unite as one humanity. With the knowledge that each person has value and a purpose regardless of race, religion, social status, financial position, or any level of hierarchy or separation. We can then look inward and focus on being the change we seek to see in the world from that place.

Quote

"Always be a first-rate version of yourself rather than settle for being a second-rate version of somebody else, for somebody else." Judy Garland

Admiration of a Visionary Leader

Diane immensely admires and has followed Patricia Cota-Robles as a beacon of light. Patricia has been a leader in the Lightworkers Community for over 35 years. The sacred knowledge that Patricia brings forward has greatly assisted Diane in stepping out of traditional ways of thinking and stepping up into God's work. Through an expanded understanding of the bigger picture unfolding on the Earth at this time. Patricia's work centers on a heart-based perspective. We are all God's children and all divine in nature regardless of how far off the path we may have wandered.

Patricia's leadership and work have taught Diane that there is always a higher truth to our experience no matter our mistakes in our human journey. As co-creators in our life, we can continually transform our lives into something more aligned and more purposeful. Sometimes we need someone to shine that light for us and illuminate that which we ourselves cannot see.

Diane sees herself as a visionary leader. She is committed to assisting others in gaining clarity, confidence, and understanding of their true nature. She is sharing guidance on navigating these incredible, though often challenging times, that we are facing today on Earth.

Journey of Discovering the Greatness Within

Diane learned early in life that if you started to form a habit of settling in any area of your life, in time, you would be settling in all areas of your life. She learned that people of high stature were some of the most dysfunctional people that she knew, and for that reason, she started out in life not wanting to be like them. You know the people with money, the well-dressed (snobs) at church whose behavior didn't match the message of Christ that she was being guided by. Those that put profit before people, or whose entire identity is attached to their material wealth (mostly debt), were people she steered away from.

Diane recognized that people who seemed the most judgmental were the ones she disliked the most. She realized that just because her parents wanted her to be good at something, it was not always a natural fit. She learned that the more they pushed her towards things they wanted her to excel at, the farther her interest would be in pursuing what they wanted her to do.

She remembers deciding that there were two kinds of people in the world at a very young age. There were people who taught her what she wanted to be like, who lived their life from a more heart-centered place, who were naturally kind (like her grandfather), whose focus was people's well-being, rather than material gain and possession. Particularly when for example, money was used as a payment or reward for bad behavior, of which she saw plenty.

She learned that there were also people who showed her what she didn't want to be like. Some of these people displayed abusive behavior, were selfish, self-centered, or were downright inappropriate towards others. Many people, often seen as the ones doing good deeds at church, were the ones most guilty of causing harm, be it physical, mental, or emotional, to their children, spouse, or community. These became some of the things Diane spoke out against her whole life. She believes that all abuse is unacceptable.

Seeing these differences empowered Diane to stop using excessive alcohol and drugs, which she was introduced to at a very young age. It caused her to take a solid step back in her early twenties and begin to look at the world through an expanded set of eyes and led her to want to learn everything she could about things like distant healing, reincarnation, energy fields, the Laws of the Universe, and so much more.

Through this new lens, Diane learned more and more that settling was something that people with poor self-esteem did. That settling was often related to beliefs, be they conscious or unconscious, that did not serve our highest good or our true purpose.

She learned that if you let people treat you poorly, you were, in essence, permitting them to do so by allowing their poor behavior to continue. She learned that people needed to look within and not place their focus outside of themselves, be it on other people or circumstances. When you lift the veil to the truth, the lesson is always about us and for us. Through Diane's tireless work in the Radical Forgiveness framework, she learned to look in the mirror. Looking in the mirror, both literally and proverbially, was a valuable exercise she could put into practice because it was an empowering and effective way for change to take place from within.

For most of her life, a driving force for Diane has been setting healthy boundaries and standing up for her beliefs. She learned that there are no victims in this thing we call life and that playing the part of the victim only made her feel like she was a hostage to outside influences and people. Settling never brings anything but more of the same to itself. It is Universal Law.

Diane has studied and gained certifications, knowledge, and understanding for over thirty years. She now shares this knowledge while she assists those she works with and those she loves, and it is how she lives life daily. She strives to live from a place, knowing that life holds much more meaning than what appears on the surface. We are all a bit like an iceberg with more unseen parts to ourselves than seen, which encompasses our whole being.

Empowering Results

One of the most effective ways Diane found to help someone was to ask, "How can I be of service today?"

How can she help this person feel better about themselves or their circumstances, even if only in some small way? She learned that her gift was to provide women with a safe place to be themselves, share their deepest fears, and identify their true heart's desires. This has been one of the most rewarding and fulfilling aspects of Diane's life.

The Importance of Women's Contributions

Diane advocates for speaking the truth, even when it is uncomfortable to hear. She has always stood by the belief that the truth allows us to make informed and educated choices and decisions.

Diane had to make choices that were not popular with those around her when she chose not to do any chemotherapy after being diagnosed with breast cancer in 2007 and 2009.

During that difficult time, Diane faced ridicule from people she sought guidance from. As well, she had to try and help alleviate other people's fears and opinions. She stood firm in her belief! Going down the pharmaceutical route did not align with her beliefs of overcoming this health challenge.

She was scorned by medical professionals who disagreed with her decision. Regardless of how uncomfortable it became, Diane never budged. Her decision was to use an alternate route, which included relying on her immune system and her relationship with God to get her through.

Diane feels that as a woman in today's world, we are the nurturers of not only our families and our communities but of our souls as well. She believes the feminine aspect of ourselves needs to be tapped into and acknowledged on a much deeper level as we embody the heart energy for the planet.

Many of our fears are programmed into us. Women can best support one another by rising above the ego and facing our fears versus denying them.

When we see others as competition, we are creating an outcome based on lack - rather than abundance.

By letting go of the negative energy of competition, we can move into the positive energy of collaboration.

Greatest Achievement

Diane's greatest achievement is one of not settling for situations that did not feel right to her soul. She gained strength in not allowing people to intimidate her about her choices, regardless of how strongly they felt. She built that muscle up by not settling for less than her worth in her jobs, relationships, and, most importantly, her health.

An Inclusive and Diverse World

Since a young age, Diane has held in her hip pocket a profound tip that encourages us to show up as the best versions of ourselves. Her go-to statement has for a long time has been 'Nothing Heals in Denial.' Suppose we deny there is something to heal, improve upon, or change. In that case, we will never move the needle in the direction of a solution to align with the best version of ourselves. We are setting ourselves up for failure by choosing to deny a problem exists.

Secondly, she has taught her clients that growth and change are always an inside job. When we project fault and blame on everything outside of ourselves, whether we think it is the government's fault, banks, markets, family, relatives, spouse, children, the boss, we are placing ourselves at the mercy of everything outside ourselves. This is disempowering on so many levels.

The third most valuable piece of advice she can share is that settling is an energy that will always bring more of the same. Once you do it once, the ego will always find ways and reasons why you should do it over and over again. When you use words such as: I don't want to rock the boat, I don't like confrontation, there are no other jobs out there, I don't want to hurt someone, so I will take a backseat again to keep the peace.

You are saying to yourself; I am not worthy of anything greater than this when you make excuses to stay in unhealthy situations and less than joyful experiences. Over time that leads to feeling jaded, disrespected, not heard, or valued. Start building up a new muscle that says I am no longer settling for anything that doesn't feel right to my heart and soul.

 Number four is to practice; yes, it takes practice to tap into and confidently follow your intuition. Diane is an Intuitive Channel whose gift is being a conduit to bring guidance and messages to you from your higher self. She has learned that people are afraid to trust their gut for fear of making a mistake. They would rather hire a coach, a reader, or phone a friend than go with their gut. You cannot expect an unused muscle to be strong enough to carry you through life's ups and downs.

Number five is to use your voice to speak what is true for you without the need for approval from anyone else. To align your actions and your intentions to be in sync. An example would be that you are working on being less judgmental, and your nosey neighbor stops in, and you immediately engage in gossip. In the Law of Vibrational Match, this gossip becomes a doorway for that judgmental energy to come straight back at you. When we begin to embrace this truth, we become more cognitive of our actions, words, and intentions.

Strategies to Succeed in Our COVID Changed World

In today's challenging landscape, what has helped Diane is having faith in an outcome that leads humanity into union vs. separation. She believes that our choices lead us in one of two directions. They either lead us towards our divinity or away from our divinity. Separation, segregation, and division are not God's way. Allowing the government, media, and medical professionals to determine your choice is extremely disempowering to the soul, which then leads people away from divinity and their God-given power.

She believes that medical choices are as individual and unique as our soul and that each of us is entitled to do what feels right for us as sovereign beings. She stands for inclusion and uniting with humanity and does not let the fear porn, the media, or 'people she doesn't want to be like' rule her choices.

Author's Quote

Freedom of the human spirit. Diane has a quote on social media right now that says, "I am much more concerned about your freedom than I am about your opinion" because that is what is at stake. She also believes that another personal quote she has lived by for as long back as she can recall has never been more important than it is right now. Her go-to statement for a long time has been, "Nothing Heals in Denial."

If we deny any problem exists, it cannot be improved upon or changed. When our fear of facing it is bigger than our faith to overcome it, you can be sure you are going away from our divinity!

Bio

Diane is an Akashic Record Consultant, Intuitive Channel, and Work from Home Business Mentor specializing in Life and Soul Purpose information and guidance.

Diane spent over 20 years in Senior and Executive Administration while filling her passion for Spiritual Studies which allowed her to travel North America advancing her certifications and interests in Reiki, Quantum Field Healing, Soul Readings, and the Akashic Records, as well as having a home business and all the benefits that go along with that.

She loves helping people fire their boss, follow their heart's desires, and the letters and feedback she gets from her clients on how their lives have been changed for the better is the most rewarding piece for Diane. Whether it reads my journey is so much clearer now Diane, or I stood up for myself today, or I picked a lane, and it is amazing what it did for me, Woohoo I made my first sale. They all raise Diane's joy vibration!

If you would like a copy of her Free E-Book "The Divine Truth - How to Receive Guidance From Your Soul" by Diane Lang

Email: beyondbeautywithdiane@gmail.com

(Please put Divine Truth E-Book in the subject line)

Join Diane's Community and Facebook Group at Awaken Your Inner Warrior

Follow Diane on Facebook at:

www.facebook.com/beyondbeautywithdiane

BIRTHING YOUR PASSION

Chapter 5

Passionate Purser of Purpose

Amber Ann Lyon

CEO & Founder of From Pain to Purpose, Inc

Introduction

Amber Ann Lyons' life's work is to help people transition from a place of pain to live in their purpose by embracing healthy relationship skills. Amber is the CEO & Founder of From Pain To Purpose, Inc.

Her very life is a testimony of From Pain To Purpose! Amber's work in the Healing Pain Through the Arts Youth Program is acknowledged nationally and globally. This has elevated her to the Global Leader of the World Women Conference & Awards and Young Leaders Club under the leadership of the Ragne Sinikas. She is diligently working to rebuild a village of support for our youth and create collaborative opportunities to position them for leadership success.

Mission

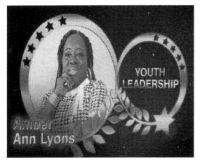

Together as a village, a community, we embrace and share the skills of healthy relationships and build a future for our youth.

Amber is globally acknowledged and known as the "Queen of Smooches" for her authentic, loving spirit and vibrant personality. She is an ordained Elder, intercessory prayer leader, podcast host/producer, author, and global youth leader. She displays a fiery passion as a transformational speaker who speaks out against domestic violence and advocates for youth.

Mission Statement: To provide resources, tools, and support to assist adults and youth with life transformation from past pain to living in their true purpose through healing from the inside out!

Vision

With all the resources within the Global Leader of the World Women Conference and Awards and the Young Leaders Club, she has a network to build her vision which is vital to our upcoming generation of youth leaders. With a vision of impacting one million youth positively, she is well on her way.

Vision Statement: To mobilize a global community of women, men, and youth who will work together and rebuild the village, which is vital to the success of our upcoming generation of youth leaders by empowering their voices to impact this world positively.

Quote

"When they go low, we go high." by Michelle Obama, because in life, situations and people will try to take you down with them, but always seek to rise above.

Admiration of a Visionary Leader

The Visionary Leader who Amber admires is the former FLOTUS, Michelle Obama. She is a woman of color. As the first African American First Lady, she never disappoints the young black girls and women who see her on a stage, on television, or in magazines. She exemplified the epitome of class, dignity, integrity, and strong character yet showed humility in caring about others. Amber always says that "People don't care how much you know until they know how much you care." Michelle walked by her husband's side, the former 44th President of the United States, Barack Obama, as a woman who demonstrated her influence and strength. While also balancing seemingly with grace; Motherhood, and an amazing career. What is Michelle wearing? Let's not forget the elegance and fashion style that everyone was drawn to. Her work with young girls and even her Move-On Program for Youth to integrate more healthy lunches into the school system could also be seen that came from her heart. Her quote, "When they go low, we go high," is one of my favorite quotes. Let's face it, that in itself takes great discipline of oneself; sometimes people will make you not want to take the high road. But, those words ring true as a reminder that you are better than going low to return evil for evil.

Journey of Discovering the Greatness Within

As a young, bright-eyed girl from Brooklyn, New York, Amber's teachers always said: "Amber is a very smart girl… and very talkative." Who knew that one day, God would use her gift of using her voice to empower, educate, equip, and encourage people on a local and global level? Wow! Well, that young, bright-eyed young girl's life took many turns and even some detours to bring her where she is today. Whew! You know people always say, "If you only knew my story, or you don't know my story!" Well, either way, you say it; it is true, but one thing that she can declare is that; God Gets All the Glory! Life has a way of being prophetic if we only follow the path that God has designed and specifically carved out for our lives.

Amber left college due to pregnancy with her oldest daughter (who is an amazing businesswoman, wife, and mother with her own phenomenal family). Amber married the father because she was pregnant. She often said she would never force her daughters to get married if they became pregnant outside of marriage. Why compound one problem with two? Getting married was not in her plans at that time, but nonetheless, that is what occurred. After being a young mother and divorced within two years, let's just say this was not on her list of life goals. She was the best mother she could be at the young tender age of just two months before her 20th birthday. The fantastic thing about it is that they kind of grew up together.

Fast forward to many years later, when her daughter was six years old, Amber remarried and believed that they did everything God's way… THIS TIME! Amber was a born-again believer, an ordained minister, and very involved in ministry by this time in her life, so to do marriage the right way meant everything to her. Haven't you heard that bad things happen to good people all the time? Well, who is to say that bad things won't happen to you just because you do the right thing? Who would think being married to another minister would end in divorce after almost 20 years of marriage with two children together (a mother of three talented children)? They were both elevated in ministry to a higher calling of service; she was an ordained pastor, and he was an ordained elder. She never expected to walk down that road again, a twice-divorced woman of God serving in leadership in ministry… Jesus! The pain that filled her soul was more than she could bear. Even her children wanted her to get a divorce. Still, she stayed and prayed while she kept trying to believe God, even amidst several separations. One day, she woke up and realized that she was living beneath her privilege. She never wanted to be divorced AGAIN. But it was not God's will for her to remain in an unhealthy, toxic marriage living a life filled with pain and emotional turmoil.

An opportunity presented itself for her and her children to receive counseling and other helpful resources. She remained in counseling for one and a half years and her son for three years before they relocated to Atlanta, Georgia, to rebuild their lives from ground zero. Both of her daughters were already residing there.

Amber was one of the most successful clients of the New York City Family Justice Center under the Mayor's Office to Combat Domestic Violence. In gratitude, she volunteered to give back to women and children suffering in silence for a year. The center sent her to San Antonio, Texas, for Domestic Violence Advocacy Training. In attendance were all levels of government, law enforcement, medical, advocates, and every organization supporting domestic violence victims. At this training, God birthed her non-profit organization, From Pain To Purpose, Inc., which began her advocacy in community work.

Revelations 21:4-5a, And God shall wipe away all tears from their eyes; and there shall be no more death, neither sorrow, nor crying, neither shall there be any more pain: for the former things are passed away. And he that sat upon the throne said, Behold, I make all things new.

From Pain To Purpose, Inc. has become so much more than a local community advocacy organization for domestic violence and teen dating violence victims. They have a powerful Healing Pain Through The Arts (HPTTA) Youth Program focusing on youth advocacy, providing opportunities, resources, collaborations, media platforms, and more.

Their Youth Speak Out Podcast has grown during the COVID-19 pandemic to 5 Countries and 7 Digital Platforms. The work with HPTTA Youth Spotlight Awards has received national media attention. Their global platform has greatly expanded through the work with the World Women Conference & Awards global organization. Amber has served for the past year as the Domestic Violence & Youth

Advocate of the Atlanta Chapter and as the Global Leader of the Young Leaders Club.

That bright-eyed, smart, and talkative young girl has now empowered so many men, women, and youth to use their Healthy Voice to express themselves. This work is very important because people carry a lot of past life trauma, hurt, pain, and unforgiveness, which detours them from their true life's purpose. Forgiveness of yourself and others is key to the healing process. Working within the entertainment industry as her son's manager for many years is how the HPTTA Youth Program was birthed. Amber watched him use his love and passion for music, songwriting, acting, and performing to help heal his pain. They utilized the arts as a cathartic tool to help youth express their pain or whatever social issues concern them. Her global work with the WWCA Young Leaders Club has allowed her to create programming for youth worldwide, focusing on various topics. This year's theme: New Year * New You (Find Your Voice & Life's Choice). So many amazing open doors of collaboration, opportunities, and networking have been a tremendous blessing to continue the work that God has called her to do. So, yes, she is walking in the purpose and calling God destined from the beginning. Her life's purpose is to help as many as she can to transition From Pain To Purpose! Haven't you heard that; "It's not how you start, but how you finish!" So, never give up hope; keep going and see what the end will be… In the end, WE WIN! Nay, in all these things we are more than conquerors through him that loved us. Romans 8:37

Four Steps to Move Forward

1. Hard work does pay off, so KEEP THE FAITH! Remember that life is a marathon and not a sprint. So, take your time to learn and grow and make mistakes because they are part of your growth and development into becoming a great leader. Be mindful that Rome was not built in a day and that we live in a microwave society; 'I want it now,' which can become a roadblock to your success. So,

take the time to do the work, and all good things will come to those who wait.

2. Remain Humble! In life's climb to success, pride can become a dangerous enemy to your soul. Always treat people the way "they want to be treated," not necessarily how you want to treat them, because that may not be what they desire or need. A great leader always has an ear to hear. It's ok to celebrate your victories; just be sure to know that God gets the Glory for it all! Pride goeth before destruction, and a haughty spirit before a fall. Proverbs 16:18

3. Cultivate and maintain the heart of a servant! When you lead with a servant's heart, you are reminded that your calling is Not About You! You can be in tune with those you are leading and remain true to the assignment you have been called to fulfill. Remember, this is all about the Purpose for which you were born onto the earth. No matter what great platforms you may find yourself on, always remember that your assignment is about the cause(s), the work, the community, the world, and most of all, the people!

4. Stay connected to a great support system and never stop learning! The world we live in today is technologically driven, creative, very diverse, and rapidly moving. To be a great leader, you must continue to challenge yourself with gaining new knowledge, developing new skills while also surrounding yourself with those who can support you in these areas. No man is an island, and we all need a support system. As you receive support, be sure to be a support of others.

Empowering Results

As a mother of 3 adult children and a grandmother of 4, she is by nature a nurturer as most women are. She has provided affirmations, scriptures, and resources to provide a source of help and added strength. Amber has prayed, supported, financially supported, encouraged, and verbally counseled many women, men, and youth. They have been able to gain a new perspective regarding their life or present situations that they were dealing with, which helped them through some difficult and challenging times and life's decisions.

Always put God first because we cannot do anything without faith from a higher source that strengthens us during our weak moments. Second, believe in yourself even when others don't and share your WHY!. Third, build a strong support system to rally around you and, in turn, support others as well. Fourth, make sure you take care of yourself (self-care)! Put the oxygen mask on yourself before you try to help others. Lastly, don't forget to enjoy life and do the things that bring you joy, laughter, and happiness while making time for what truly matters, family and friends.

Amber has made a powerfully positive impact in her community through her non-profit sector work with Domestic Violence, Teen Dating Violence, and Youth Advocacy, and through her work in ministry as the Elder serving over the Leaders of our Social Media Ministry and Singles Ministry. Her voice impacts her community and abroad. She is an Intercessory Prayer Leader during the COVID-19 pandemic on a greater level than ever before, not only in her church but has been requested to pray at events in person and virtually at other churches within Georgia, other states, and around the world.

It is key and vital that women continue to add value to the world because young girls of all nationalities are looking for an example. As an African American woman of God, it is very important for her to show support to other women. Amber sees them as Queens and calls them that because it elevates them when they hear it, no matter what is going on. It is an immediate spirit booster and elevates your heart and mindset. This support is what young girls need to see and not all the negative and derogatory words used to describe women and girls today, especially on social media and within the music and entertainment industry, which negatively impacts them. She also motivates women to know that *WE ARE WINNERS No Matter What; Because Losing is Not an Option!* It is a mindset that must be embraced with all that we go through as women and the many hats worn and roles that we play. We pour out and must be reaffirmed, validated, and refilled.

Greatest Achievement

Being named the World Women VISION Awards Winner of the Youth Leadership Category in March 2021 was an accomplishment of which she is extremely humbled and proud to receive global acknowledgment for all the work that she has been blessed to do with OUR Youth.

An Inclusive and Diverse World

Walk in Your Own Superpower
Embrace Your Own Identity & Be Proud of Who You Are
Share Your Culture with Others - Educate, Equip & Empower others to do the same
Stay In Your Lane

Accept people for who they are

These methods are important for everyone to all work together for the common good of all humankind and rebuild the bridges of unity that have been torn down by racial disunity, gender bias, and so many other issues that divide and separate us. United we Stand and Divided we Fall!

With such a competitive, selfish, critical, and crab-barrel mentality that we live in, everyone just cares about themselves and not how what we do affects others. These negative behavior patterns can lead to other destructive behavior patterns that are duplicated by our younger generations, who are becoming our leaders. We must know who 'you' are; however, we must also be *willing* to deal with the negative issues that cause us to walk contrary to who God truly desires us to be… a UNITED people! The love of God and a servant's heart have helped Amber to be able to use these methods for the good of the community and the global world at large.

Strategies To Succeed in Our COVID Changed World

 Amber and her team successfully pivoted to Virtual Platforms for their Youth Speak Out Podcast - Live Streaming Bi-Weekly. They remained consistent during the entire pandemic from March through December 2020. In January 2021, they changed directions again. They returned to meeting in-studio to pre-record for editing and uploading on YouTube & Digital Streaming platforms. The podcast has grown globally to 5 Countries and 7 Digital Platforms in addition to the amazing growing team of Co-Hosts.

Amber was honored to spearhead the coordination of a COVID-19 Youth Awareness Roundtable Discussion for the WWCA Atlanta Chapter as the Domestic Violence & Youth Advocate. This socially distanced in-person event successfully provided a safe space for youth to discuss their pandemic experiences. The amazing Youth Speak Out Podcast Team facilitated this. Youth were validated and given an ear to Hear them, Heed them, and Help them!

September 25, 2021, was a Highlight for the Youth Speak Out Podcast Team, where they did a phenomenal job as the Hosts of the HPTTA Youth Spotlight Awards. This in-person event honored Youth who have remained resilient during the COVID-19 pandemic.

The Grind Don't Stop is another one of her mantras and sayings. Determination is key to obtain any level of success that you are striving for. Be determined to remain resilient during a time of crisis in our changing world.

Author's Quote

"Make It Do What It Do!" No matter what happens in life, we have to remember that; if we, do it from our heart and unto God, it will work out, so do your best and leave God the rest. And whatsoever ye do, do it heartily, as to the Lord, and not unto men. Colossians 3:23

Bio

Amber Ann Lyons is the C.E.O. & Founder of From Pain To Purpose, Inc. She invites you to support our youth and build our worldwide village. She is an ordained Elder, intercessory prayer leader, podcast host/producer, author, and global youth leader.

The work with Amber's Youth Spotlight Awards has received national media, and their global platform has greatly expanded through their work with the World Women Conference & Awards global organization. She has served for the past year as the Domestic Violence & Youth Advocate of the Atlanta Chapter and also as the Global Leader of the Young Leaders Club. That bright-eyed, smart, and talkative young girl has now empowered so many men, women, and youth to use their Healthy Voice to express themselves.

Amber would like to dedicate this chapter to her 3 Children; NaQwanna Thomas (Shaun Thomas; Son in love), Janelle Lyons, and Emmanuel Lyons, as well as her beautiful 4 Grandchildren, who bring so much Sunshine to her life (Torian & Teigan Thomas and Zy'Air and Zyauna Ratley). These are her *Legacy Carriers*, and she is grateful to have their love and support over the many years. Amber also dedicates this chapter to all of her family, friends, and supporters who have supported her throughout the years. She is humbled and grateful.

Learn more about this author

Thank you for reading her story. Amber prays that it has impacted you to seek to pursue purpose with a renewed passion. Don't merely exist but become intentional about fulfilling the God-given assignment all that you have within you. The rest is up to God. It would be an honor to have you contact Amber via her social media platforms or email provided in the code below. **Let's Connect and Pursue Purpose Together!**

Social Media links

https://linktr.ee/alyons63

Chapter 6

My Pain Birthed My Purpose

Rosalind Willis, PhD.

Co-founder of "T&R Birthing Books Publishing LLC"

Introduction

Coach Roz is your birthing purpose coach. She assists individuals in discovering their God-given purpose and walking in it. She believes that if you have a pulse, you have a purpose in this earth realm. Your fingerprints prove that you are a unique design because no one in the world has your prints. As a coach, she can help you identify what that purpose is and come off mute to find your voice.

Dr. Rosalind Willis (Coach Roz) Dr. Willis is a stroke and domestic violence survivor and advocate. Dr. Willis has a passion for serving and reaching the lost at any cost. She is the Co-founder of "T&R Birthing Books Publishing LLC" and is an international public speaker and published author. She is the Founder of BOMI Ladies Club Global Empowerment Movement

Mission

Dr. Rosalind says she is not here to compete with you but to complete others! Dr. Rosalind is the Birthing Purpose Coach. Coach Roz holds local events called Ladies Tea every three months. She brings ladies together to offer them coaching to help them get unstuck. Coach Roz offers workshops and deliverance to build up self-esteem or whatever the woman needs. The big focus is to heal the total woman. Dr. Rosalind is also a publisher and published author of 11 books, and Coach Roz teaches women how to write books. She hosts a writing boot camp.

Mission Statement: To take her empowerment teams worldwide, helping women by providing tools, encouraging, and supporting them, changing the world one person at a time with love!

She is changing the world, one woman at a time, through nourishment, encouragement, and empowerment. She loves every woman and knows we need each other to survive.

Vision Statement: To see every broken woman she encounters become whole.

When women come to Coach Roz, they are broken, especially when they come through our Ladies Teas. We can then do one-on-one coaching. We also do a deliverance service. We help women get rid of the things that have broken them, such as a broken marriage or relationship, so that they can deal with those issues. We provide referrals for people that need a little bit more help. We work with them to help them heal by offering resources to help them with finances and things that factor into a purposeful life and get back to a place of wholeness.

"If you don't like something, change it. If you can't change it, change your attitude." Maya Angelou

Admiration of a Visionary Leader

Dr. Rosalind Willis admires every woman who has come before her paving the way that led her to become the woman she is today. First, she is thankful for her mother for being a teen mom and giving birth to her when she could have abandoned or aborted her. Dr. Willis honors her mother for loving and teaching her how to love hard and embrace everyone regardless of color or financial status; her love never stops. Her mommy is her heart.

Secondly, she is grateful to her great grandmother, the late Beatrice Clark, for passing her the prayer and ministry mantle. As a little girl, Dr. Rosalind remembers her praying and standing in the gap for others. She still recalls the things her grandmother spoke about that she now walks in today.

Third, her Aunt Sylvia Moore has always been a second mom to her, and her love and support have never wavered.

Lastly, she would say Oprah Winfrey is the visionary leader. Dr. Rosalind admires the following qualities: Oprah is an encourager, a born leader, a champion of women like herself, and Oprah supports women's rights helping to give them a voice. In this beautiful world we live in, there are so many more women to honor, but Dr. Willis will stop here for the sake of space. However, she wants to honor every beautiful woman that picks up this book and wants to remind you to PUSH! BE EVERYTHING GOD CREATED YOU TO BE!

Journey Of Discovering the Greatness Within

Dr. Rosalind Willis's story starts with her being a high school dropout because she had to help her mom and dad.

Being the eldest of her siblings, Rosalind had to work full time while going to school when both her parents became ill. She never thought twice about it. She always considered herself sacrificial. Once her dad recovered, her parents started a restaurant. Dr. Rosalind was always good at waiting tables and customer service because she loved people and loved to serve. She always thought of others before herself.

Dr. Rosalind became a teen mom at the age of 18. She always dreamed of having her own business from her youth because she saw the freedom it gave her parents. She learned how to start a business and run it from top to bottom. This is where her entrepreneurial passion was planted. No matter what she did, Dr. Rosalind always felt she had missed out because she was not able to graduate from high school with her friends and family. Someone along the way told her that she could never go to college with a GED. So, she had in her mind that she would never get to walk the stage and get a degree. After giving birth to her son, she began to think about how she wanted what was best for him. Even though she worked full time and now had her own place, she wanted to give her son a better life than she had.

She got married and moved to Georgia. Her first husband was in the military. She went through a lot but felt blessed with a beautiful son and daughter. The marriage ended in divorce. However, God blessed her with a bonus daughter through her ex-husband's extramarital affair. In the midst of all this, God was with her. In 1995 she answered the call of ministry. By this time, she was praying, motivating, and ministering to everyone that would listen.

But she was not taking care of herself. Mentally, emotionally, and physically Dr. Willis was broken, and only God could fix her. She did not love herself; that was the root of her problem. She had been abused mentally, emotionally, and physically; she felt she was a mess. But God healed her, delivered her, and revealed himself to her. She went back to school and received her Bachelors,

Masters, and finally her Doctorate while being a single mother of three kids.

After all these years, God blessed her again. Her first husband, her first love, found his way back to her. At this time, she wrote out her vision and made it a plan for every dream she had.

Seven years ago, Dr. Willis had a stroke because she worked full-time in ministry giving to others and did not exercise self-care. While recovering in the ICU, God gave her the vision to empower and build up the women in her community. She wrote down God's message line by line how he gave it to her.

Dr. Willis now arranges empowerment teas and has been for seven years, and they are life-changing for those that attend. They are successful and very impactful. This year's tea party events went global, and in 2022, her tea party events will be held in different USA cities and London. She gives God all the Glory.

Dr. Willis has stayed committed to what God has given her to do. Put God first, and he will direct your path. Without Jesus, Dr. Willis can do nothing, but all things are possible with him. Dr. Willis now feels healed, whole, and focused on her vision. Stay true to yourself and know your worth.

Life dishes out many roadblocks, but our job is to work past these and grow from the experiences—some steps you can take to improve your outcome of life's challenges.

The first step is self-care; make sure that you are taking care of yourself. Make sure that you are eating right, exercising, and resting. Your health truly is your wealth. Please take your spiritual prenatal vitamins if you are pregnant with a promise as you are birthing a vision.

Second step is writing out your vision, your short and long-term goals, and making a plan that is easy to understand. This is important because if you cannot clearly understand it, you cannot explain it to a lender, partner, investor or see it clearly yourself. You must visualize your baby.

Third step is to protect your vision. You cannot share your vision with everyone because someone can steal it from you and make it their own if you have not done the proper paperwork. It is like giving birth; you cannot show your baby to everyone.

Fourth step is to focus on your vision until you see it come to pass. Giving up is not an option, no matter how hard it gets. Remember, you are the only one that can feel your baby kick, so do not let anyone talk you out of your vision. It is your time!

Empowering Results

One of the ways Dr. Willis has empowered and nurtured others is in her Empowerment Tea events. A woman who attended her event provided a testimonial that she was on drugs but was delivered during a Tea Party event and has been drug-free now for five years. She shared that she did not have custody of her kids because of her drug use; today, she has all four of her children, married and drug-free.

Dr. Rosalind Willis is a caring person who serves people in many ways. She motivates them with love and encouragement. Dr. Wills shares and teaches her life coaching skills and book writing classes.

Dr. Willis is affectionately known as Coach Roz. She hosts a talk show called Keeping it Real with Coach Roz where she comes off mute and invites women to tell their stories and step into their destiny. Everything she does is motivated by love, and that is the key.

In Dr. Rosalind's community, she helps women who have lost all hope to find and obtain hope again. She has served hundreds of women through her Empowerment Tea outreach that she holds every three months. She has hundreds of ladies' testimonies saying their lives were changed at her Empowerment Tea events, and they will never be the same. There was a lady in attendance at a tea that had not cried in 9 years was numb as she lost her son in a car wreck. She came to our tea and experienced a breakthrough. A year later, she is a Certified Grief Coach helping other women who have lost their children or are experiencing sickness. Lives are definitely being changed.

It is always important for women to add value to the world. Dr. Willis supports women by offering them a shoulder and an ear. She supports women by giving them tools to help them find and birth their purpose. She provides a masterclass to teach skills they may not have, such as computer skills, budgeting, parenting classes, or whatever their need is. She also supports women by giving them platforms.

Greatest Achievement

Her greatest achievement is her Ladies Tea. Women who attend these tea events find their purpose, which is the main focus; helping women understand why they were put on this Earth. They provide workshops offering group coaching and 1-on-1 coaching if they need intense support to help them achieve their goals. Suppose a woman wants to be an entrepreneur or develop a particular skill. In that case, the Ladies Tea workshops offer training or refer them to other places where they can gain specialized training. If any woman wants to get back into school or find employment, we help them find solutions and answers to their problems.

Dr. Rosalind has followed God's plan and continues to do so through her Ladies Empowerment Tea Party events. At these events, women come together, and through encouragement, support, and various tools, they can experience life-altering changes.

An Inclusive and Diverse World

Every three months, Dr. Willis holds ladies' tea outreach events. She uses the following tools and practices to bring in sisters from all over, and the love and encouragement there is evident in the faces of everyone.

Practice 1: Promote sisterhood and embrace our unique differences by bringing together women from all walks of life.

Practice 2: She promotes and teaches self-love, self-care and gives women the tools they need to unlock their full potential.

Practice 3: Checking your pulse - Dr. Willis teaches that you have a purpose if you have a pulse.

Practice 4: Dr. Willis teaches women to value their unique differences. She has them look at their fingerprints and reminds them that no one in the world has the same prints as they do!

Practice 5: This is the practice of love, as it has no color, and when we focus on love, the colors disappear.

Check out the pictures of our last tea; it was a very diverse and beautiful group as always. She loves to serve these beautiful jewels.

Strategies To Succeed in Our COVID Changed World

Dr. Willis calls the tools she uses "repackaging." She has been teaching masterclasses in person for years and has a curriculum set up for face-to-face instruction. During COVID, she had to learn new skills. She learned how to work with Zoom and Streamyard to offer her classes on those two platforms and conduct interviews and host meetings. Dr. Willis now has a YouTube University.

Determination is important for success because it fuels your rocket to launch you into your purpose. We must use that fuel to ignite the passion for our purpose to become the best version of ourselves.

Author's Quote

"As long as you have a pulse, you have a purpose" by Dr. Rosalind Willis

Bio

Dr. Rosalind L. Willis: aka "Coach Roz is an International Public Speaker, Global Leader, Global Ambassador, Domestic Violence Survivor, and Advocate, wife, mother of 6, and Nana of 13. Ordained Evangelist for 27 years who loves outreach ministry. Dr. Willis is a ministry educator and CEO of several businesses. She is the Founder of BPMI Ladies Club Global Outreach. A Non-profit Organization that brings women from all walks of life together to help, support, uplift, and give them life skills and tools to improve their lives. She is a member of the International Society of Female Professionals, a U.S. Representative for Birland A New Country, the Texas Chapter Leader for WWCA, the Lubbock State Chair for G100 Oneness & Wisdom Wing, Global Ambassador for TGA, BPMI LADIES CLUB GLOBAL, and Global Diversity Leader for Face of Women of Hearts.

Dr. Rosalind is the Global Executive Director for Celina Fashion International Magazine

Connect with me

https://flowcode.com/p/Ppk7P6RTS?fc=0

SUCCESSFUL CARING, CONNECTING, AND EMPOWERING

Chapter 7

Successful Caring Connector Who Is Inspirational and Resourceful

Viola Edward

Co-Founder-Owner of GRIT Academy

Introduction

You are just one breath away from support in your personal and business life. Viola provides and assists you with clarity through sustained success by connecting amazing humans to one another, leading to life-changing opportunities.

Since the nineties, Viola has been a pioneer in developing mental health fitness and emotional well-being in the workplace through a cross-pollination method that bridges the space between our differences. Through mentoring, leadership, and Breathwork, she helps management and staff find the road to self-improvement and sustainable productivity.

Viola has had an unusual awareness since childhood. She finds inspiration from people and is curious about human behavior and how challenges affect achievements in life.

Viola professionally uses her experiences and knowledge to help others around the globe to reach the best version of themselves and to have clarity toward their success.

Mission

Viola is a woman living a meaningful and loving life. She has been on a continuous path of growth. When sharing a part of her story, Viola remembers, she has been a migrant frequently in her life, recreating herself each time. Exploring, learning, and expanding in a sustainable way has been her passion since 13, when she interrupted her formal schooling and started working for a living. Her non-formal education has been and still is her best companion. Having led her to the delight of creating teaching spaces that enable people to develop, grow and sustain, individually and in groups.

Viola professionally uses her experiences and knowledge to help others around the globe.

Mission Statement: To provide wide-reaching teaching spaces and educational services through non-formal education, enabling people to develop, grow, and sustain as individuals and groups.

Through Viola's personal experiences, she now shares and helps others live a better life, enjoy rewarding relationships and find their passion.

Viola shares her methodologies online and offline with thousands and is a multi-awarded advisor, author of two books, and co-author of thirteen more. She is a spontaneous relational being - gifted with intuition and curiosity. Wherever life leads her, Viola knows she will be able to cope with the situation, own it and use it as a beneficial learning experience.

Vision Statement: To help build a world where people can lead more peaceful and balanced lives where healing, service, and human values are at the heart of all things and touch all people, and where justice and equality exist for all.

Quote

"You cannot get through a single day without having an impact on the world around you. What you do makes a difference, and you have to decide what kind of difference you want to make."

Jane Goodall

Admiration of a Visionary Leader

Viola found inspiration from a Visionary Woman that she knew very well. Her name is Rose, Mama Rosa for many - Viola's mother.

Rose was 24 years old when she became a widow. Her darling husband, a musician by heart and an engineer by profession, passed away at 29 after a heart attack.

Tragically and suddenly, Rose found herself in a foreign country, seven months pregnant and alone with a 3-year-old daughter -Viola. Rose was in a dire and dramatic financial situation, in shock and scared, but Rose was there all the time for her children. Her resilience, love, care, and her big vision came through for them as she had a clear vision of how and where it would be safe for her children.

Rose was resourceful and reconnected with her natural resources through relationships and service to others. She found creative ways to feed and clothe her children. Her love for cooking, fashion, and looking good combined with her imagination got them through tough times. She recycled everything, sewed their clothes, and created wonderful meals based on her cooking love.

Rose raised her children with love and instilled enduring life-sustaining characteristics so they would thrive.

Viola's darling mother worked with a smile until her last breath and always gave generously. By Viola's good fortune, she inherited many of her mom's resourcefulness and skills. As her mum, Viola reconnected with her natural resources through relationships, service to others, and put her several languages to good use. Viola shines at connecting people and has the capacity to integrate ideas and people. She is caring, intelligent, hardworking, creative, positive, grateful, and resilient.

Journey of Discovering the Greatness Within

Viola started her working life at the age of thirteen when she migrated with her mother and sister from Lebanon to Venezuela. She fed her passion for development and study through homeschooling, evening lessons, and alternative educational pathways. She has become a multi-awarded personal advisor, transcultural psychotherapist, Breathwork mentoring /trainer, social entrepreneur, business consultant B. and humanitarian.

In 1993, with twenty-one years of experience working in the corporate environment, she renounced her career as a successful marketing manager to follow her dream of becoming a Psychotherapist and Breathwork Trainer. Viola was thirty-four years old when she broke free, pursuing her dream beyond habitual bounds, daring to open her heart and let the metal of her grit come to the surface. As a result of her studies in Transpersonal Psychotherapy and then Breathwork from founder Leonard Orr, she realized that breath was at the core of every person's well-being, a discovery she was eager to share with others.

She has been pioneering and developing mental health fitness and Emotional well-being in the workplace since the nineties, bridging the space between Breathwork therapy and business management. She now works internationally with individual and corporate clients in a cross-pollination between self-development, management, and leadership. As a creative entrepreneur, she is a synergist, developing innovative schemes. She recently introduced Breathwork to rehabilitation from addiction, a theme in her life that she successfully overcame.

Sixty-two years old Viola is a multiple-award winner, including - Doctorate Honoris Causa, Aspirational Woman, and Outstanding Contribution to Mentoring. She is the author of two books: - "Breathing the Rhythm of Success," "Who Makes the Bed?" and co-author of 13 more.

She is the CEO, Co-founder-owner of GRIT Academy, Partner of Creative Women Platform. The Co-creator of the BQ- Breath Intelligence and GRIT Breathwork Method. Viola also sits on the boards of several magazines and NGOs and serves as ambassador for Human Rights and Gender Equity.

Viola is a woman living a meaningful and loving life. She has been on a continuous path of growth, and when sharing a part of her story, she says: "I have been a migrant frequently in my life, recreating myself each time. Exploring, learning, and expanding in a sustainable way has been my passion since 13 when I interrupted my formal schooling and started working for a living. Non-formal education has been and still is my best companion, having led me to the delight of creating teaching spaces which enable people to develop, grow and sustain, individually and in groups".

Viola's clients and colleagues call her "Master Mentor and Connector." She is particularly valued for her intuition, experience, integrity, and creativity. Her motto is "Together is Better for Caring Alliances."

Important steps that Viola shares:

7 steps for your personal and professional life:

1- Get a mentor and a psychotherapist, heal whatever is remaining from the pain and the losses of the past. Invest time, energy, and space; you are important.

2- Create or review your vision and mission and create a set of goals and go-to action plan.

3- Develop a routine of what you like the most, singing, journaling, meditation, walking, yoga, dancing, reading… and enjoy the set that you create, tailored-made for you; when the time arrives, you can add or change whatever is needed.

4- Set boundaries in time in your relationship

5- Be thankful and move on

6- Honor the healthy trait of your personality

7- Continue your self-improvement personal and professional

7 steps for your loving relationship

1- Love
2- Communication
3- Healthy sexuality
4- Core values hold in common
5- Some shared interests and hobbies
6- Agreement in the distribution of duties (especially the ones that none of the two like)
7- Continuous learning and healing individually and in partnership

Empowering Results

In many ways, Viola is a Mentor by profession and by heart. Viola helps others get out of the cognitive blindness, shorten the curve of learning, interact, and create maps with their clients. She even gives out a connection list, whatever is needed to support others professionally while adhering to loving professional boundaries. Viola has traveled with her clients, gone to their weddings, and visited them in the hospital if needed.

Viola enjoys a great conscious loving relationship with her lover-husband-friend Michael. They met in 1999, they have lived together since 2002. They work together supporting couples in their journey at their Kayana center on the north shore of Cyprus.

In addition to her love for her mother (her hero) and her husband, the big and wide love in Viola's life is her darling sister; they are friends and partners. "She is an amazing woman, multi-talented, creative, caring, and compassionate."

Viola's life and work with her husband and sister are very important for her. It is crucial to remember that working with family members is possible and wonderful, just as it is important to heal any remaining family traumas. "Not everybody can work with family members. But if you have the chance, go for it. It is sustainable and can be a synergy of love to create effectiveness in your business, entrepreneurship, and the causes that you are engaged with."

What are some Innovative and Outstanding ways you motivate?

Women need to acknowledge themselves and set boundaries in their relationships ON TIME. When boundaries are communicated on time, they can be soft and gentle, and the couple can learn from it; when boundaries are left for later, they will come out harder, and the damage is bigger too.

As soon as women learn this, a huge percentage of their problems will ease.

Viola extends the thought that it is crucial that women exchange the perfection ideal for the excellence ideal. Perfection is a huge enemy for our daily life and most professions. Let's also agree that women do support other women; it is not a matter of gender; some personalities are more individualistic and not at ease supporting others. It can happen with both genders. Please do ask for help, do not leave your doubts and pain alone. Count on me.

What positive impact have you made in your community? *

Viola has worked with thousands of people, using her practical methods to help them unlock the infinite possibilities hidden in each of them and find the courage to start their own journey to achieve their full potential.

Viola has touched many hearts and souls, and here are two examples of how her love, care, and compassion have embraced others.

"…The day I met her, I loved her. Later I loved her because it was easy for me to feel her love. I loved her more for her devotion to others without borders of time or space. I continued to love her when I was helpless, and she sheltered me among her people; I loved her for the patience of her faith in me."

Sonia Pirona - Poet, Journalist, Chef

"…I was searching for help with my way of being. The first thing that struck me about Viola was her modesty in conveying her wisdom with simplicity and depth. I then discovered her commitment and passion, truly connecting with people, her innate ability to 'accompany them' during their process."

Yolanda Farrais - Breathworker, Lecturer

Viola is the creator of Feminine Capital Rhythm, which has two pillars.

The first pillar is a program designed for women to rediscover themselves, their rhythm, and their power. These discoveries help balance the light and the shadow of their feminine and masculine energies, bringing equilibrium to their families, colleagues, and communities.

The second pillar was an international forum presenting speakers & panelists on different areas of life. These forums focus on empowering women to embrace their femininity and men their masculinity to break free and create a more sustainable society. The forum gives inspirational awards to outstanding people, and the first successful event was in Cyprus in May 2017.

In 2020, Viola joined the FCF into the 'Creative Women Platform" as a partner and Executive Director to strengthen her work and network with women worldwide. Also, Viola is the Ambassador, Honorary Chairperson, consultant, or Board member of several networks for women such as - Charity on Wheels, empowering the forgotten population - women in prison, -S H E - Sociedad Hispanas Emprendedoras", -Mujer Ideal, -WEDO: Women Entrepreneurship Day, -LOANI -Ladies of All Nations International-, iWIN - International Women in Intensive & Critical Care Network

- W4S Women for Solution for a Caring Economy, - WWCA World Women Conference & Awards, - Female Civility, - WAW Women Appreciating Women, - Female Wave of Change, -SIMA, She Inspires Me Awards, - WWE World Women Empowerment,

- WICCI - Women's Indian Chamber of Commerce and Industry, among others.

Greatest Achievement

Visionary women often have many achievements, and Viola is no exception as she has had to reinvent herself several times. Learning a new language is often a great achievement which Viola has done a few times. Still, her greatest achievement would be healing from within. Viola has recovered from addictions, learned so much, and keeps learning every day. She has healed the victimhood of the grief and losses that life delivered to her.

"In my youth, books were my refuge, but what really saved my life in addition to the love of my family was the powerful combination of psychotherapy, Breathwork, and my love for humanity." Viola Edward

An Inclusive and Diverse World

Viola is the honorary president/chairwoman, vice-president, board member, and representative of twenty non-profit organizations and foundations. One of them helps Women in prisons. Viola is part of a 3-month program of Gender Parity that is given for free in several countries or at the cost of $5. They recognize and acknowledge women from around the world. She is part of a team through the International Breathwork Foundation working for Breathing Day to be recognized in the UN. She also works in various institutions with the SDGs, the Sustainable Development Goals of the United Nations mainly focus on numbers -3-Good health and well-being, -4-Quality Education, -5-Gender Equality, -16-Peace, Justice and Strong Institutions, and -17-Partnership to Achieve the Goals, so No-one is Left Behind.

Through her books, Viola reaches a diverse public, a note to the reader

"...What does it mean to be in a deep, loving, conscious relationship? How does one get there? What is conscious communication, and how can we achieve it? What is healthy sexuality? Here you will find the answers to these and many more questions, written in clear, helpful prose, by someone who 'walks the talk.' The book "Who Makes the Bed?" offers wonderful pointers and guidelines born of Viola's deeply personal experience and vast therapeutic knowledge. This book is for anyone who is in a relationship, or out of a relationship, or starting a relationship, or who simply is dreaming of having one… it is filled with fearless honesty and passion for helping others discover their essence, which is the hallmark of Viola's work. Love, wisdom, and enthusiasm permeate every word within these pages." Endorsement by Guillermo (Willi) Ricken - Creative Entrepreneur

Strategies to Succeed in Our COVID Changed World

Viola and her sister Layla created the GRIT Academy during COVID.

GRIT is an acronym of GROW-RESOURCE-INSPIRE-TRANSFORM- it is an accessible, rewarding, and life-transforming program. They have been focusing on the meaningful and long-lasting transformation of 1000's of lives since 1993. During COVID, they were ready to share their knowledge and legacy on a global scale with GRIT Academy.

Above what they already did, Viola and her sister created two more programs. The first one is the GRIT Star. It is a live interactive seven-session program conducted in small groups where every participant's journey and transformation are important. Implemented with simplicity, GRIT Star takes the participants through personal and professional growth, benefiting their lives and the lives of others. They support their growth with flow, enthusiasm, humor, and integrity.

The 2nd program is the GRIT Coach/Mentor professional training, an intensive 85+ hours program. This prepares all participants who did the first level and would like to take it as a profession to provide the GRIT Star program in their communities and language and be trained as Mentor and Coach or improve their skills.

In GRIT Academy, they welcome anyone and everyone. Both sisters are relational and value connections within their community. They embody what they teach and are focused on raising the level of consciousness while supporting sustainability and growth on a global scale. The programs will be taught in several languages: English, Spanish, Turkish, Arabic, Russian, French, and Greek.

Scholarships in their programs are available to support as many people as possible.

Would you mind looking into their programs at www.gritacademy.co and helping them improve the world? There are discounts and scholarships for the programs, and they are free for people in need.

Viola professionally uses her experiences and knowledge to help others around the globe. She is thankful and healthy, with many loving people around her, and is certainly at service for humanity.

"Another star in my life is the beauty of Breathwork. That is when wealth is really there! It is a vital connection, guiding her to be fully in the 'here and now,' healthy and free of limitations."

Author's Quote

"Where we are breathing, we are alive, and where there is life, there are infinite possibilities!" Viola Edward

Life can be very challenging. But if we understand the power of life and the power of breath, we will be able to move on and surprise ourselves with the whole world of our infinite possibilities to expand, to serve, and thrive.

Bio

Viola Edward is a multi-awarded Master Mentor & Connector, Advisor to leaders and organizations across multiple sectors, Transcultural Psychotherapist, Strategist, Lead Trainer of Breathwork, Mentoring, and Coaching. Business Consultant B. Co-Founder-owner of GRIT Academy & Partner-ED of Creative Women Platform. Co-owner of Kayana Center. Board Member. Pioneer of Mental Health and Emotional Wellness in the workplace since the early nineties and since then engaged with a Sustainable Society.

Viola is the co-creator of BQ- Breath Intelligence and GRIT method: Grow-Resource-Inspire-Transform. She is serving as an ambassador for Human Rights and Women Equity. She speaks English, Spanish & Arabic.

Author of 2 books, "Breathing the Rhythm of Success" and the Amazon Best Seller "Who Makes the Bed?" plus a co-author of 13 more books.

If you feel Viola can support you or your business, she is just one breath away,

connect her … https://linktr.ee/ViolaEdward

Learn more about this author

Get my books on Amazon; they are both in English and Spanish, read them and do the exercises, contact me for support, and join us in GRITAcademy.co, there is a program just for you. Please subscribe to my YouTube Channel and enjoy the interviews with inspirational leaders and my own lessons. Download my eBook from my website BQ-Breath Intelligence and do the evaluation and the exercises; connect with me for more.

Viola Edward
CEO Co-founder
GRIT Academy
00357998751094
info@violaedward.com
info@gritacademy.co
www.violaedward.com
www.gritacademy.co

Chapter 8

Connect, Inspire and Empower Women Worldwide

Maria Renee Davila
the CEO of the Global Trade Chamber

Introduction

Maria-Renee is the CEO of the Global Trade Chamber, an international chamber helping entrepreneurs and companies start, grow, and explore new global markets. This Multi-award winner has received public recognition from local, national, and foreign governments, Non-Public Organizations, and various multi-national companies. She is the Founder of the 100 Successful Women in Business Network that empowers, inspires, connects, and recognizes women worldwide. She's an International Business Trainer and International Speaker.

Mission

Maria Renee and her team develop and implement global events, programs, multimedia tools, including digital marketing, TV shows, magazines, books, and branding.

These services enable women from many nations to share their stories, promote their organizations, empower, and inspire others and connect to other amazing women from many nations and industries.

Mission Statement: To connect, educate, and promote women in business and women entrepreneurs worldwide and bring together women of different ethnicities celebrating each other with a vow to embrace and encourage one another.

Vision

Maria Renee and her company are mentors, teachers, and coaches for women of all ages to start and grow a successful organization.

Vision Statement: Be the leaders in connecting women entrepreneurs worldwide and helping them compete and succeed in constantly changing global markets.

"I don't go by the rule book. I lead from the heart, not the head." Princess Diana

Admiration of a Visionary Leader

Maria Renee sees Margaret Thatcher, former Prime Minister of the United Kingdom as a visionary leader. She was the first woman to hold that office. Maria Renee admires her because of the uncompromising leadership style that made her a strong world leader and respected by many. She implemented a series of economic policies to reverse high inflation and struggles during a recession. Maria Renee has overcome many obstacles as a woman CEO in chambers of commerce. She has implemented several programs to help women from many nations to learn how to be women leaders and impact their communities.

Journey of Discovering the Greatness Within

Maria Renee was born in Bolivia, where she began her modeling career at 12 years old. She participated in a fashion show as one of the models and won a scholarship to study modeling. That was the starting point of her modeling career. At 17, she asked her mom for help to start her company. Opening her first company was not easy at all. Because of her young age, companies did not take her seriously or believe she represented models, managed an academy, or organized events. One of the biggest challenges was looking for sponsors, as they did not take her seriously. It was so bad that she had to take her mom with her to talk on her behalf, sign contracts, and pick up checks.

At one point, she got very discouraged, but somehow, she picked herself up and did not quit. Her company grew and became extremely popular. With time she expanded her services to video production and others. Maria Renee had fortune 500 companies and government agencies as clients. She contributed to several mass media channels (TV, radio, newspaper). Unfortunately, as her company grew, her challenges also grew--delayed payments from clients, the competition underpricing services, political unrest in the country, models breaking contracts, etc. Her mind and body were tired from working over 60 hours per week between the office and events on weekends.

After ten years, she decided to sell her company and move to the U.S. with her husband. Starting a new life in America was a total shock for her. She did not know the language or the culture. She went from being totally dependent on herself to starting over in a new country. A terrible depression set in that was so bad she returned to Bolivia. She felt lost, not sure what to do with her life. Her father told her to go back to the U.S. and study something. Taking his advice, she returned to the

U.S. to attend the American Intercontinental University, where she got a Master of Business Administration degree. Studying in another country in another language was incredibly challenging as well, but she did it!

As Maria Renee built confidence, she got the opportunity to work with and for companies as an international event planner traveling overseas for events, plus became a faculty member for several universities. She learned the importance of networking and building relationships to move ahead in life. Her entrepreneurial spirit helped her overcome many challenges, including sexual harassment, discrimination as a woman, and Hispanic Women in Business.

For over 14 years, she has been helping companies start, grow, and succeed in local/global markets. Their many services include international events, trade missions, virtual offices, digital magazines, Live Streaming TV channels, webinars, seminars, and conventions. Their global network gives them a tremendous reach to many markets. Their vision is to connect businesspeople worldwide. Three years ago, she created the 100 Successful Women in Business Network to connect, empower, inspire, teach, and recognize global women in business.

Maria Renee is honored and humbled to have received public recognition and awards from local, national, and international organizations for her service and inspiration to many entrepreneurs and young people in many nations. Her life has been the life of an international entrepreneur since the age of 17; there is no goal or challenge too big she cannot reach. The world is getting smaller and the opportunities bigger; the only limits you have are the ones you put on yourself.

Empowering Results

As a chamber CEO, university professor, mentor, and coach, Maria Renee has worked with many students and members of the chamber, advising them on ways to have a balanced life and how to start and grow successful enterprises around the globe.

Maria Renee Davila has empowered women around the world by collaborating on a book series called the 100 Most Successful Women Around the World, plus giving them a platform to speak so that they can share their amazing stories on how they moved from struggles to success.

She also coaches' women on marketing strategies so successful women can scale and take their business to the next level.

Maria Renee helps women gain visibility and exposure on various platforms she has founded, such as the 100 Most Successful Women Book series, Successful Business in Magazine, Global Trade Chamber, an organization that connects buyers and sellers worldwide. Through her organizations, they find amazing everyday successful women making positive contributions in many fields, including education, politics, and corporations.

Greatest Achievement

Maria Renee's greatest achievement in business has been to create the 100 Successful Women Network connecting, teaching, empowering, recognizing, and inspiring women around the globe. Along with this achievement, she launched the 100 Most Successful Women Around the World Book, The Successful Women in Business Magazine, and Success Stories TV Show.

An Inclusive and Diverse World

1. Networking. Constantly networking at various events in several cities to build relationships, grow our network and find new clients.
2. Digital Marketing. Implement several digital marketing tools, including social media, digital magazines, online TV, online events, and webinars

to market and promote our services to clients across the world.
3. Alliances are crucial to any organization. They help multiply our efforts to expand to new markets and reach new people.
4. Education. It is a very important part of everything they do, working with international universities and industry experts to keep entrepreneurs up to date on the latest information to start and grow successful businesses.
5. Consulting. Their team of experienced experts in many fields provides consulting to businesses enabling them to compete in global markets.

Strategies to Succeed in Our COVID Changed World

Maria Renee implemented several digital tools to help her connect with other people worldwide. Such as magazines, Online TV channels, virtual events, virtual meetings. This was an opportunity to connect with successful global leaders worldwide and help them connect with others, so together, we explore, network, and support each other's business.

Author's Quote

"The only limitations you have are the ones you place on yourself." Maria Renee Davila

Bio

Maria-Renee Davila is a proven international entrepreneur with extensive corporate experience and solid leadership skills. She started her career when she was 17 years old. With over 15 years of experience, she has also served as a director for other companies and worked with Fortune 500 companies. She provided consulting and resources enabling companies to succeed in local and international markets by developing a marketing plan, business plan, market research, and business training. Managed and produced world-class business events, including International Business Expos, Trade Missions, Fashion Shows, and International Conferences for alternative energy initiatives, biofuels, government, nonprofit organizations, and privately held multi-national corporations in several countries. CEO of the Global Trade Chamber, Co-founder of the 100 Successful Women in Business, Past Board Member of Latin Women Business Organization. University Professor in South Florida teaching Business Administration courses including International Marketing, Marketing Management, Marketing Communications, Public Relations, Labor Relations, Business Management, and Sales Management. Speaker at workshops to businesspeople, community leaders, and students on various topics. She has received public recognition from local, national, and foreign governments, Non-Public Organizations, and various multi-national companies for successfully executing events. Also, she has been interviewed and featured on magazine covers and international publications and was a TV host and model.

Some of the Awards she received.

Hispanic Leaders Award from the city of North Miami 2018

50 Most Powerful Global Trade Advocate by the US Department of Commerce and the MBDA Export Center 2019

100 Successful Women in Business Award -2019

Where People Need People - Unity in Service 2019

Ladies of All Nations Global Award -2020

Recognition for helping women around the world by Miss International World Organization 2020

Mandela Medal - World Peace Award 2021

Lifetime Achievement Award from President Biden 2021

Learn more about this author

Do you have something to offer the reader? What would you like the reader to do next?

(Get your E-Book, watch a webinar or join your Facebook group).

The 100 Most Successful Women Around the World

Provide contact information

Maria-Renee Davila, MBA

CEO- Global Trade Chamber

Co-Founder 100 Successful Women in Business

Business Trainer - Higher Education Professor

mariarenee@globaltradechamber.com

www.globaltradechamber.com

https://www.youtube.com/c/Globaltradechamber

Facebook pages

https://www.facebook.com/globaltchamber

https://www.facebook.com/100successfulwomeninbusiness

https://www.facebook.com/groups/463221724992884

Chapter 9

Succeeding Without Boundaries

Sarifa Alonto-Younes, EdD

CEO & Founder of Arndell Park Early Childhood Learning
Centre

Introduction

Everything that you have today and everything you can be
is due, in part, to those who came before you. Meaning:
the amazing women of the day have a role in shaping who
you are and who you may become.

Since 2007, Sarifa has been helping and empowering
orphans, disadvantaged children, and women. She has been
sponsoring more than 500 orphans and underprivileged
children's basic needs and education from 3rd world
countries like the Philippines, Cambodia, Vietnam,
Uganda, Liberia, Zimbabwe, etc. Currently, she is in the
process of expanding her orphanage facilities in the
Philippines to provide shelter for 300 orphaned girls and
accommodate for their educational needs.   She is also
sponsoring bright university students from marginalized
populations to achieve their university degrees.

She believes that gifting education is a very powerful tool to empower and eradicate violence and poverty. This support helps women develop financial independence and sustainable skills through different projects and social media platforms.

Sarifa is a philanthropist and a serial edupreneur who has been coaching and mentoring women so they can climb up the organizational ladder. She is an international speaker who inspires, educates, and empowers women to realize their potential and talents, bringing out their leadership abilities.

Mission

It has been Sarifa's mission and purpose in this life to focus and exert her energy into inspiring, empowering, and transforming disadvantaged women all over the planet. Born in this era of advanced knowledge, she constantly strives to reach out to women through global means. She is helping them achieve self-awareness of their true strength and guiding them to their true purpose through self-transformation. She wants them to become leaders in their own right.

She has assisted many disadvantaged women in becoming financially sustainable by providing monetary help to learn sewing, weaving, and beading skills. Sarifa would be their first customer, encouraging them to become more independent and sustainable. Sarifa inspires other empowered women to provide and empower disadvantaged women to be part of a solution instead of burdening society.

Mission Statement: is to empower and transform disadvantaged women and girls into global leaders through education and self-awareness.

Sarifa educates and empowers women and the young generation to bring out their leadership skills.

Vision

Sarifa's vision is to live in a world where educated, empowered women and girls acknowledge and understand their potential and abilities. So, they can be inspired and develop the self-confidence required to succeed in their life journey and become independent, empowered, and effective leaders.

Educating and empowering a person today is creating an immeasurable investment for tomorrow.

Quote

"Education is the passport to the future, for tomorrow belongs to those who prepare for it today." - Malcolm X

"The content of a book holds the power of education, and it is with this power that can shape our future and change lives."- Malala Yousafzai

"The ability to read, write and analyze; the confidence to stand up and demand justice and equality; the qualifications and connections to get your foot in the door and take your seat at the table – all of that starts with education" - Michelle Obama

Admiration of a Visionary Leader

Sarifa admires Oprah Winfrey, a woman who's been there – and rose above it all. Oprah grew and overcame the obstacles life presented to her by finding lessons in those around her. She is now one of the most influential women you see today.

Sarifa shares a message from Oprah about setting limits:

"Every time you state what you want or believe, you're the first to hear it. It's a message to both you and others about what you think is possible. Don't put a ceiling on yourself. Take a look at where you are and your surroundings. You had a hand in getting to where you are. And you also have a hand in where you go next."

Oprah came from humble beginnings, born on a tiny farm in Mississippi in 1954. Living in poverty and being a black woman in the American South, facing harsh obstacles before her teenage years.

Nothing could stop her drive to become more, and by 1986, she was the first black female host of a syndicated daily talk show. By 2003, she became the first black female billionaire in the United States. And in 2011, she launched her TV network. If you find that you're outside of your comfort zone and need inspiration, Oprah's story is full of secrets to success. She's changed the lives of millions, both through her show and her outstanding charitable efforts.

You're still writing your story no matter where you are in life. You are in charge of where you go and how you get there.

Are you going to learn to embrace those challenges and strip away limits like Oprah? Success starts and ends with your mindset. This amazing woman learned to embrace who she was and how her journey will help others on theirs. It is hard work growing into your potential. But you can do it if you're willing to push through your obstacles.

Sarifa's admiration of Oprah Winfrey is because they both went through the same experience of struggles. They both learned lessons from those around them and challenged themselves to turn struggles into opportunities to achieve their dreams. When there is a will, there is a way! But the most important thing is to be thankful and grateful for whatever you have and share your blessings whenever you can.

Sarifa grew up as an orphan, losing her father at the age of three, and her mother lost her battle with cancer when Sarifa was only ten. Sarifa had to learn how to push harder than others to move forward and achieve her goals.

She learned to love the countless obstacles in different shapes and forms that crossed her path.

Journey Of Discovering the Greatness Within

Sarifa was armed with nothing but a dream. A dream to end her misery and get an education. The first step was teaching herself to read and write from her brother's schoolbooks, then plowing through a series of obstacles, prejudices, and gender inequalities was next. She recognized those challenges and confronted them head-on turning them into opportunities. Studying hard to continue her education as her mother used to tell her, "Education will drag you out of misery." Her mother's words of wisdom served as a reminder to keep her focused whenever her emotions swayed her off track.

Along Sarifa's journey, she learned and realized that there are no limits to what she could achieve. With every passing year, she became more and more empowered. Slowly but surely, she managed to claw her way up into leadership positions and become a serial entrepreneur. This may never have existed if she had been unwilling to take risks and push through the obstacles years ago.

When you are grateful, your heart is full of joy and happiness. This permits your positive hormones to build up to a certain level to sustain your growth mindset. That growth mindset can lead you to the pathway to paradise.

Finding that road to greatness isn't always easy. Sometimes you run into obstacles that seem insurmountable. No matter how hard you try, they threaten to knock you off your path. So instead of railing against these obstacles, learn to embrace them. Even the most powerful women in the world didn't get there overnight. They had plenty of obstacles of their own to overcome. But if there's one thing that Sarifa's experience imparts, it's that growth happens outside of a comfort zone.

Empowering Results

Sarifa has owned a business for more than eighteen years, allowing her to help and nurture many women to bring out the leaders in them. Each of them is different, and she celebrates those differences. She invites them to share their views because each of them matters, and their opinion is important to the business's success.

Supporting these women in their journey is very important for Sarifa. She encourages them to share their personal stories so she can help them both personally and professionally. It makes it easier to coach and mentor them when she knows their stories.

The nature of Sarifa's work inspires her to help prepare young women to develop their skills and talents. She draws strength and inspiration when she nurtures and mentors young women while helping them realize their potential and making them responsible and accountable for what they do. They can then intelligently participate in decision-making at home and the workplace, regardless of drama and draining emotions.

Promoting and training some of her young employees to C-Suite (C-suite are executive positions CEO, CFO, COO, and CIO) positions is a blessing for her and more than enough to be thankful and grateful. So far, Sarifa has assisted nineteen students in completing their university degrees!

Sarifa has been actively engaging in inspiring women without even realizing it since February 2004, eighteen years ago, and it's just the beginning of her journey.

She has established a few educational institutions in Australia and the Philippines to serve the communities and provide quality education for the young generations.

Education is empowering, and through learning, young generations of women's skills are enhanced. They are equipped with the ability to acquire other new skills allowing them to progress and grow personally and professionally.

Establishing dedicated spaces for women creates an area to share and celebrate each other. Bringing people together forms a sense of unity and improves the flow of information. It lets women know, "We are all in this together."

Each of us has a role to play, and we must know and understand our strengths and talents to add value to the world. We can be supportive of women in many ways. Leading by example can inspire a new generation of female leaders. Hiring and developing female talent are essential steps to promoting female leadership.

Sarifa has been looking for ways to create more job opportunities for women for years through establishing educational institutions. This allows her to employ and train more women to C-suite levels. Then mentoring and coaching them, so they acquire the necessary skills and knowledge to perform their jobs effectively. Women are integral for shaping our world. Likewise, we are integral in shaping the world for them and future generations.

Greatest Achievement

Sarifa's greatest achievement in life was obtaining a quality education in the field of psychology and education (Bachelor in Psychology; Masters Degree in

Industrial and Organizational Psychology; Masters in Education and Training & Doctorate in Education, Ph.DH). She was orphaned at ten years old and thought it would be impossible for her to complete even her primary school. When she completed her education, she vowed to help orphans and disadvantaged children access education. She was so grateful, and that's when she realized that succeeding has no barrier (nothing is impossible) when we have the WILL to succeed.

An Inclusive and Diverse World

Today, she is the president, CEO, serial founder, edupreneur (entrepreneur in education) /entrepreneur, philanthropist, speaker, mentor, and coach to many women in Australia and the Philippines. Sarifa is the recipient of multiple awards. A winner locally and globally made her realize that she needed to play her role in being part of a solution. She now is making a difference by paving the way for the next generations to come.

Sarifa has four beautiful children with whom she ensures spending quality time and is married to a supportive husband. Having them in her life is a blessing.

She is grateful to have achieved so many dreams using her ADD (Accept, Decide, and Dream) formula. In her #1 best-selling book, Love Your Obstacles, she talked about it in detail that she has unconsciously implemented since childhood.

Sarifa shares her practices to harness the power of diversity and inclusion that leads to innovation.

1. First, having a support system in place for women of diversity is very important for their professional and personal growth. Without a strong support system, you have only yourself to rely on.

2. The power of women's communities is in collaboration, networking, and strong collective support. Women are naturally good at nurturing and motivating each other. When other women surround us, we get the strength to uplift, inspire and empower each other, and we experience collective success.

Sarifa wishes she had connected with communities of empowered women earlier in life. Although still thankful that it is not too late to connect, collaborate, and network with those amazing women who are making a difference.

3. Women make great role models and create interest while exploring what makes them tick. They dig deep to become the best version of themselves that they can be. Women are natural nurturers, so we need to take other women under our wing when we are in a position to do so, especially in an industry that's notorious for creating gender barriers for advancement.

The beauty of role modeling is that women fall naturally into that role and should not be afraid to be role models for the wanted changes. They're more likely to empathize with others who struggle with the same things that they did. And they're more likely to help.

4. Women in leadership roles are naturally inspirational within their organization. They already leveraged their strengths and weaknesses to get to where they are today. But why stop there when you can inspire and empower many women of diversity, so they become included? Help unlock higher performance potential in other women.

Anybody can be an inspirational leader if they focus on what they do best.

5. Unconscious bias on a general level becomes more dangerous when it evolves into gender bias. When someone has a gender bias, they will pass over one gender to the opposite gender. Often, women are biased against because some believe they can't contribute as much as the male gender. Women should arm themselves with indisputable facts to confront this type of bias. Use the quality of your performance to demonstrate that you're a capable leader. Nobody can deny the numbers.

Strategies to Succeed in Our COVID Changed World

Just about everything in Sarifa's life changed at first when the obstacle of the COVID-19 pandemic sent the world into lockdown. She felt restricted, unproductive, and stagnant—no choice but to stay at home.

She knew this obstacle was just another challenge to overcome and began by restructuring her daily routine to accommodate both family and work. It was not easy in the beginning to transition from being physically outside of the house during working days to being locked in 24 hours a day.

Acceptance was a potent tool during the COVID-19 pandemic. By accepting the situation, she became more flexible. She began the transition to her new life, which she DECIDED to shift to a digital platform while being with her family and spend some time working on some unfulfilled DREAMS that required her attention.

She was thankful her childcare and kindergarten center were still operating to support parents—the essential frontline workers such as supermarket staff, nurses, pharmacists, and medical doctors.

She took advantage of being at home and utilized the time to prepare for the years to come, including spending more quality time with family. Sarifa got to know and understand her husband and children better, seeing their flaws, strengths, abilities and guiding them where needed.

She also wrote her second book, The Future of Women in Leadership, scheduled to be published in 2022.

Sarifa adapted to a new routine of working from home. She ensured her work and her schools continued to receive the attention they deserved. But she continued her typical daily routines of personal care and exercise.

During the COVID-19 pandemic, super typhoons hit and devastated the Philippines, and she helped more orphans and families.

One of her innovative and outstanding ways to motivate other women to achieve success is her TALL principle, an acronym for Trust, Acknowledge, Listen, and Love.

Sarifa TRUSTs she can lead an organization and likewise trusts that her people are the right ones for the job and respects and understands where they come from.

Acknowledging the strengths and weaknesses of the staff members helps the organization grow. She ACKNOWLEDGES their achievements, strengths, weaknesses, limitations and capitalizes on their strengths. Areas that need improvement, she provides training.

LISTEN to the staff members. Sarifa knows they care, so it is vital to recognize their contribution and give them the required time and attention when they speak up. Listen to understand what is happening as they are her eyes and see things that she does not.

Lastly, she LOVES them because they are like her family. "Our workplace is a second home for all of us." People who work from their hearts treat their workplaces with care and respect. In return, they perform with so much love and appreciation. So, they deserve to be loved and respected, which makes them feel motivated and inspired to come to work.

By adapting her TALL principle, those women in our workplace feel motivated and succeed in what they do.

Without Trust, nothing begins. Without Love, everything ends.

Author's Quote

"We lead to create more leaders" Sarifa Alonto Younes

Achievements and success can only be meaningful when they make a significant difference and change a soul for the betterment of humanity and society." Sarifa Alonto Younes

Bio

Sarifa Alonto-Younes is an award-winning International Speaker, Edupreneur, Best-Selling Author, and philanthropist. She advocates for women's empowerment, education, leadership skills and is the Global Director of Speakers Tribe Women, Australia, the Australia Country Chair on Business Networking under the auspices of ALL Ladies League.

Sarifa is the CEO and Founder of Arndell Park Early Childhood Learning Centre, Melbourne, Australia; President and Founder of International Academy of Marawi (I AM), Philippines; Director and Co-Founder Training College of Australia (TCA).

Sarifa has won multiple awards, including the Australia 2018 AusMumpreneur Multicultural Business Excellence Award; the UK WOHA 2020 Mother Theresa Award; 2021 Philanthropy Award, World Women Vision Awards, and nominated for Philanthropy Award Category in WWCA.

Sarifa and her husband Hassan reside in Melbourne, Australia, with their four children and have established three travel agencies.

In her #1 best-selling book, Love Your Obstacles, she shares with the readers how she overcame different forms and shapes of obstacles when orphaned at a very tender young age of 10. She further sheds light on her life journey and how she became who she is today, hoping that some people may resonate with her story and learn from her strategies. Her book received an honorary mention at Golden Door 2021-Truth & Integrity of the Written Word. Also, awarded a Bronze Medal at Golden Door-REX Karmaveer Truth-Writer Fellowship & Chakra Awards, which is instituted by iCongo and in partnership with United Nations.

Learn more about this author

1. Get an E-book chapter of her book, Love Your Obstacles
2. Join her Facebook group
3. Follow her on social media:
4. Website: https://www.sarifayounes.com

Facebook: https://www.facebook.com/sarifaalontoyounes

Blog: https://www.sarifayounes.com/blog-1

LinkedIn: http://linkedin.com/in/sarifa-alonto-younes-455060116

Instagram: https://www.instagram.com/sarifayounes/

YouTube: https:www.youtube.com/Sarifa Alonto-Younes

INNOVATION APPROACH

Chapter 10

Innovative Approach to Achieving the Improbable

Carmen Franco

Inclusion Leader Expert in Ground-Breaking Inclusive Practices

Introduction

Carmen Franco has worked with people of all ages born with a physical or cognitive disability or experienced an accident or illness that led them to be physically or cognitively impaired. Carmen has an unyielding resolve to find fulfillment for her students. This has led her to believe that we can all discover our inner purpose and live our lives to achieve ultimate life satisfaction. Life goals are attainable when you have the right approach, and Carmen is dedicated to finding that approach. When you can understand yourself without pretense or criticism, you can begin to see the world in a different light.

Mission

Carmen is an educator creating inclusive classrooms for students with disabilities to give them a sense of belonging. She wants to ensure diversity and inclusion for generations to come, improve innovation, motivate collaboration, and increase our future leaders' self-esteem and confidence.

Mission Statement: is to uplift the underrepresented by freeing them of the proverbial chain and setting them down a pathway they didn't know existed.

Vision

Carmen Franco is a student of theory and focused on improving educational practices to impact students with special needs. Carmen is empowering students' abilities and inclusion to cultivate excellence to create awareness of individual needs, shape attitudes, and cultivate positive results for all students.

Vision: Spaces where people accept a person for who they are, exactly at that moment. That's the world Carmen sees when she closes her eyes. In this space, it is understood that where there is potential for growth, there is also room for acceptance.

Quote

"Do one thing today that scares you - and you already know what that is! - and go do it. Even if you just make one step toward it, it will help you look at the world differently."

Luvvie Ajayi Jones

Admiration of a Visionary Leader

Dr. Maya Angelou is a visionary, a woman, and a leader. When Dr. Angelou was curious- she learned. When she thought something unjust- she fought for change. Her innovative spirit and unyielding optimism led her from one opportunity to the next. Carmen learned many lessons from her books, and she believes in approaching obstacles with optimism and innovation.

Journey of Discovering the Greatness Within

Carmen Franco was born in Corpus Christi, Texas. Growing up in South Texas was rich in culture but often mundane. She lived in a rural area outside a small town of 1,212 people and has rarely met a person who grew up in a smaller town. Carmen couldn't wait to graduate high school and leave that town. She wanted to get as far away as possible and hoped to attend college in Hawaii. However, life had a different path for her, and as Carmen's family experienced hardship - she had to alter her plans. She decided to attend the University of North Texas in Denton, Texas. She received a master's degree from Texas Woman's University. Upon graduation, she took a job in Fort Worth, Texas, and remained in the Fort Worth Independent School District for ten years. She has learned many things and has become a leader in her field. She hopes to continue to grow and positively influence people along the way.

In Carmen's small town in South Texas, there was a line of division; although invisible, it was palpable for those attuned to its vibrations. Carmen fell on both sides of it in her case, for her mother is white, and her father is Mexican. Carmen remembers hearing whispers about her heritage, **her parents being both**, about her father being Mexican. The words get stuck in people's mouths like a pecan that has gone bad. Carmen's whiteness was advantageous, however, and they all knew it. Her friends of color would encourage her to talk to the teacher on their behalf. These friends would rely on her to tell their story in hopes of a better outcome. Carmen learned to manipulate truths to benefit everyone, not understanding why teachers chose her to recite truths. Yet, if this difference in her wasn't enough, Carmen knew there was something else under the surface of her being that was different, more severe, less ideal.

When she was 15, she discovered that tug in her stomach to be her sexuality. As the child of two teachers in a town where being a teacher was similar to being a celebrity, her sexuality became a problem. At a young age, Carmen was aware of perception and how it "meant everything" to her mother. She learned about that when her father had an affair which resulted in a child. Carmen remembers being told that we do not talk about that to anyone. Carmen was eight years old when she was expected to keep this quiet. She felt the pang of betrayal to her mother as she shared this secret, knowing full well others would read this story.

When Carmen realized she was gay, she knew she could not let anyone find out. Carmen had to appear perfect, just like her family had always appeared - perfect. They were a family of five, her mother a teacher, father a coach, and the three girls who were smart, pretty, and athletic. Until one day, while Carmen was a sophomore in high school, an investigation was launched on her father. Three girls had alleged he sexually assaulted them. One of the girls was so close to her family she was like a sister. It shocked the town, the school, and mostly Carmen's soul. However, Carmen was torn. She never trusted her father after the affair but did not think he was the type to do something like *that.* Yet, why would this girl lie? How could she lie about something so severe? As time pressed on and facts were revealed, Carmen knew and believed her father to be innocent of this crime.

During Carmen's sophomore and junior years, her family prepared for her father's trial. Carmen intensely felt that she had to be perfect, that her gayness was sure to be the demise of her father's case. Her biggest fear was being called to the stand as a witness and having to testify about her sexuality. Fear and anger grew steadily in her heart. Carmen soon began to act out and to drink heavily. She tried drugs, even did cocaine in a bathroom stall. By the end of her junior year, she suggested to her parents that they move. Carmen had lived in that town her entire life but knew that if she had to endure one more year there feeling the way she did, she would not make it out alive. And so, they moved, and while Carmen was free of some of the anger, she was still angry and hurt and coped using copious amounts of alcohol.

Carmen was gay, lost, and angry, and no one came to aide her.

Carmen loved to read. It turns out she absorbed life-saving knowledge and drew her resolve from reading authors like Maya Angelou, James McBride, and books about Holocaust survivors. She made it to college then almost gave up after her first year to join the Coast Guard until she was hired as a mentor with the America Reads program. This program changed her life; she found purpose and decided she wanted to be a teacher. Carmen soon began to spend all her spare time mentoring "at-risk" youth in an urban area. Carmen found something to fight for, to live for, and it altered the course of her life.

Empowering Results

Growing up, her father raised his daughters more like boys than girls. In this way, Carmen would not call herself a nurturer but a person who encourages more like a coach. She has been emboldening friends and encouraging teammates much of her life. Carmen has a unique ability to understand the strengths of a teammate and highlight those. Encourage them, not by dwelling on their shortcomings but by lifting up their strengths and never wavering in her support for them. She would pivot to turn a negative into a source of energy driving change. We each need to know that someone out there has our back. Knowing that can make all the difference in the world.

Carmen always strives to find the positives in a situation and focuses on that. Women are especially vulnerable to feelings of failure and are also often afraid to succeed. It's hard enough to compete in a "man's world," but we often fail to support each other as women. Carmen feels compelled to compliment and uplift women along their way. She strives never to compete with a fellow female, even if she feels a slight twinge of envy. Carmen thinks the best form of motivation is affirming a person's efforts, affirming their struggles, and awarding them the compliments or feedback they earn. We know success is about perseverance. With the right cheerleaders, it is much easier to step on the battlefield of life every day.

Carmen heard a parent once say, "It's hard to accept that your child will not be on the basketball team or be a cheerleader." When Carmen hears of a parent feeling distressed about things their child "cannot" do, she becomes engulfed in figuring out how to make it the seemingly impossible - possible.

Many of the students she works with are born with cognitive or physical disabilities. Some students have

an illness that leaves them with loss of brain function or an accident that changes the functionality of their bodies. Some are born with a genetic condition such as Down's Syndrome. However, Carmen has never met a student that could not achieve anything. Carmen has never settled for the idea that something was impossible, and therefore never turned away the option of hope for families. This attitude has an uplifting impact on the community. Providing space for people with disabilities within their community improves their acceptance, raises inclusive community thinking, and celebrates their wins.

This has been one of the greatest joys in her life. Carmen believes that continuing to provide opportunities for children and adults with disabilities within their community will make the world a better place - one community at a time.

The Importance of Women's Contributions

As COVID-19 has swept across the world, displacing families, eliminating jobs, and making education for many impossible- it is female-led countries that have stood out. While the research is controversial (probably because it surrounds female leaders), it does illuminate one thing, 19 out of the nearly 200 countries are female-led. Those countries female-led experienced less death than those of their neighboring male-led countries. The fact is that the sample size of female-led countries is too small to attain a good data collection, but it remains that less life was lost due to the female leaders. So, why is it important for women to achieve and add value to the world? Well, because it saves lives. Females grow life, they nourish life, and when they contribute to the community, their nation, and the world, we are all the better for it.

Carmen's support for women is vast and deep, with accomplished, strong women surrounding her. They all support each other by never doubting one another. Of course, there are always words of encouragement when needed and emotional and sometimes even physical support. But, to Carmen, the biggest detriment to ourselves as women is the doubt, we allow to creep in. Therefore, what she likes to say the most to her female friends, family, and colleagues is "yes, do it." Carmen always finds a way to shine a clear light on what can be and move the light away from all the reasons not to try.

Greatest Achievement

Carmen takes pride in herself in looking at any problem and rolling it over, perhaps ruminating, until she comes up with at least three different approaches to solving it. When Carmen taught Adapted Physical Education (APE), one barrier the APE teachers had was how to get students who are wheelchair users, to move more freely. In response to that, they developed an Aquatics program. Another hurdle they face is getting students better access to healthy opportunities, such as exercise. Carmen oversaw the development of an outreach program that allowed students with physical and cognitive disabilities to access their community recreation center as patrons, volunteers, and potential employees. Sometimes, her impact seems almost minute when looking from the vantage point of the solution phase. Still, if Carmen zooms out, she has promoted acceptance of children with physical and cognitive disabilities at their campus level and prompted acceptance from the community. Carmen has become a cheerleader for her teachers, who have picked up all the COVID-19 school years' shattered pieces and helped them form a new puzzle. She has been in the background providing tools and lending a supportive ear in the midst of it all. She has been supportive so teachers could tackle arguably the biggest hurdle of their careers, getting students back to school. This allows parents to work, provide food, shelter, and electricity for their homes.

An Inclusive and Diverse World

Carmen is an able-bodied, cisgender, lesbian female born to a light-skinned multi-cultural family. Carmen speaks English with a little broken Spanish and has been told many times in many ways that "[she] doesn't look Mexican," or she doesn't count as a lesbian because "[she] doesn't seem gay." Until recently, Carmen would listen to those words and consider herself a less than. But finally, Carmen put her foot down and said to herself, "I AM a Chicano, even though I don't look like it!" "I have experienced discrimination for being lesbian, even though I feel like my struggles don't count because of the many times I've been reduced for my looks."

Having said all that, she says:

1ST Rule is to be inclusive. You must be accepting, and acceptance does not have conditions. A person's life experiences are their own. If they tell you something unjust or discriminatory from their perspective, then it is. Whether you believe it or not and whether you can see it or not.

2nd Rule: The Power of Diversity is dependent upon allowing diversity to keep its power. Microaggressions are real. The aggressor can be unaware or aware based on their privilege, but to allow diversity to be an element for innovation, all parties need to be careful with their words and not diminish anyone's experience based on their preconceived notion. If a person feels reduced or diminished, they will not speak up to add their voice, and the project will lose a valuable perspective.

3rd Rule: Develop a safe space. Our society has narrowed down diversity into checkboxes. One can determine gender, creed, sexual orientation, culture, race, ethnicity, etc., all with a checkbox. However, not every "diversity qualifier" carries a universal experience. Therefore, do not expect people to open up about their experience just because there is "diversity training." In order for all to voice their opinions in a workspace, they must first feel safe.

4th Rule: Be comfortable with discomfort. It is human nature to want to fit in. We are a species that depends on the human connection to evolve throughout history. Therefore, in her opinion, the minority has so long tried to conform to the majority. This is especially true in the workplace. But as more courageous conversations are being held by those that have experienced discomfort, the more open people are becoming. People on the receiving end of discrimination are now speaking up and speaking out. Those in the majority are not used to hearing these conversations and feel uncomfortable, at times even offended to hear the truth. Instead of the majority lashing out or shutting down in their discomfort, it is their responsibility to listen and feel the discomfort. They need to bathe in it to fully grasp, understand, then ultimately empathize, and begin to expand their perspective.

5th Rule: Diversity and innovation evolve; we must all evolve with it. We have seen Millennials change the game during the pandemic. Computer savvy millennials have stepped up to help their fellow co-workers during this pandemic. Some Baby Boomers have had to reach out, sometimes depending on the Millennial to troubleshoot the video call or arrange a virtual conference despite not being at a senior status level. Our world is constantly evolving, and what was once "acceptable work jargon" can become insulting, harmful, and polarizing language. We live in a consumer-driven culture, and consumers expect things to improve daily. Therefore, to meet those demands, we must foster an environment that allows all innovators a safe place to shine.

Strategies to Succeed in Our COVID Changed World

In the time of COVID-19, we have all seen innovation come sweeping through with the force of a tsunami. New apps have been developed, stock in computer and gaming programs have skyrocketed, and we've seen online dating and shopping become second nature.

Of course, Carmen has utilized all the video conferencing apps and anything else that makes virtual work possible. However, in the modern spin on the classics, she has found the most comfort in, such as using a workflow app to prompt her to take a 5-minute break. During that break, she uses an app to do a short yoga practice to focus on her physical and mental health. As Carmen is stuck in the office on a computer screen, she uses one of her extra screens to stream a feed of an aquarium, to relax and view nature. Sometimes she streams an aerial view of Scotland to feel like Carmen is traveling to remember there is an entire world beyond her desk. The entire world has faced enormous hardships, but Carmen has kept these hardships in check with a determination not to lose sight of the outside world. The world beyond her office walls, or the world beyond the walls of her home, city, or country.

Determination is key to any great achievement. Sometimes our determination can be a force that helps us ignite a movement and make the impossible – attainable. And sometimes, when everything seems lost or pointless, it is our determination that says to us, "if you just get up, and make it through the day… there will be tomorrow, and you can try again." Yet, it needs to be said that Carmen has had to gather all her strength and determination many times during this pandemic just to get out of bed to do it "one more time."

Author's Quote

Understand and accept yourself without pretense or criticism and begin to see the world in a different light.

Bio

Carmen Yvonne Franco attended The University of North Texas in Denton, Texas. She received a master's degree from Texas Woman's University. Upon graduation, she took a job in Fort Worth, Texas, and remained in the Fort Worth Independent School District for ten years. She enjoys hiking, camping, and kayaking with her family. Carmen Franco is an Inclusion Leader Expert in Ground-Breaking Inclusive Practices. Her focus is to help adults and all students. Specifically, focusing on students with special needs to provide a sense of belonging and become better prepared for life, so they participate in an inclusive community as adults. Carmen believes that providing opportunities for children and adults with disabilities within their community will make the world a better place. - one community at a time. Carmen encourages all women to step into their greatness regardless of cisgender, lesbian females born to a light-skinned multi-cultural family. Stepping into who you are only empowers you to be great and become authentic

Learn more about this author

Join Our Innovative Events for PE4All

https://www.linkedin.com/in/barb-swan-wilson-9812022b/

https://www.facebook.com/barb.swanwilson

121

Chapter 11

UNEDUCATED, UNEMPLOYABLE, AND ALONE

Can a Single Mom Succeed? You Bet Your Ass She Can!

Cheryl Thibault
CEO and founder of TBO Ventures Inc

Introduction

Be certain what you ask for - You WILL get it.

Cheryl Thibault's fairy-tale dream of falling in love, getting married, having kids, and living happily ever after did not transpire. Today, 64% of women are the family's breadwinners, primarily single moms. That's where she found herself at a very young age. She was pregnant at 16, married at 17, pregnant again at 18, and divorced at 19; there she was, **uneducated, unemployable, and alone**. Her life needed a change, and she knew only she could make those changes.

Enjoy the inspiring story of her traumatic yet remarkable journey and discover what it took for her to independently go from a broke single mom to owning a global business that helps people all over the world fulfill their dreams.

Mission

Cheryl has founded several businesses, mainly salons/spas and training centers throughout Canada. She lives with a passion and purpose in all she does, setting an example for others to know that they can too.

Cheryl's Personal Mission: To Heal - Inspire - Serve, using her life, energy, love, and intuition to create change.

Vision

Strive for your dreams; they're never too small or too big. Follow your heart, listen to that tender voice inside and do what you believe is right. Never give up - even if it means making a sideways or a backward move, you will always go forwards again.

Cheryl's Personal Vision: To create a heart-led world where people come together with Love, Understanding, Compassion, and Kindness for the good of everyone. Teaching her children and now her children's children the meaning of family, core values, and integrity. The importance of what is of true value - does not hold a price tag.

Quote from a Visionary Leader

Cheryl's life has become one of caring for others, and she shares her favorite quote of a Visionary Leader with us.

"People will forget what you said, people will forget what you did, but people will never forget how you made them feel." -Maya Angelou.

Admiration of a Visionary Leader

Maya Angelou is an extraordinary woman and inspirational speaker. She appreciates where she came from and what she has gone through. This is how Cheryl also sees her life. Maya and Cheryl are women of courage who overcome and maintain a kind and loving spirit.

Cheryl lives an abundant life with the goal of a world where people come together with Love, Understanding, Compassion, and Kindness.

She shares a few steps you can take to improve your life.

- Gratitude - always be thankful for what you have
- Help others - lend a hand and always choose kindness
- One second at a time - when life gets to be too much - break it down
- In time this too shall pass

She strongly believes in the spirit of reciprocity. For as much as you are given, you must return the same to the world, trusting that it will, in turn, help someone else, knowing they will continue to bring the spirit of goodness full circle. Understanding that our path and contributions are important, then learning, and knowing that we can create anything we envision. This gives us the ability to live a rewarding and fulfilling life while creating abundance; it is a gift that can be taught and passed on.

Cheryl measures her life by the people she has touched and those who have touched hers. She loves being a positive influence on people and encourages them to strive for more.

She surrounds herself with those who share a common bond. She lives her life with purpose, always following her heart and passion.

Journey of Discovering the Greatness Within

At 12 years old, Cheryl sat with her friend, dreaming of what they would "be" when they grew up. She distinctly remembers saying she would have a boy and a girl with blonde hair and blue eyes under 2 years apart in age and be in the beauty industry doing nails and makeup. That's EXACTLY what she did. You see, when you ask for something and desire it with your whole heart, **you will get it**.

As a young adult, Cheryl found herself in a very abusive relationship. She was in a position where she was "strongly encouraged" to leave her hometown for herself and her children's safety.

Upon ending this relationship, she chose to move to British Columbia, Canada, where she currently enjoys a very active life on Vancouver Island. Her wonderful life today did not come easy; there were many setbacks, struggles, a lot of rebuilding, and finding the courage needed to go on. She knows that overcoming her challenges has made her the Visionary Leader and the Amazing Woman she is today!

There were times she *lived by the second* because living by the day or even by the hour was too overwhelming. The mantra that helped her keep going is from Dory in Finding Nemo - **"just keep swimming."**

Born in Saskatchewan, on the Canadian prairies, Cheryl was the middle child with an older and a younger brother. Cheryl was picked on and bullied by boys on the school grounds. When she expressed these incidents, she was told by authority figures it was because these boys liked her. Trusting their guidance, she learned to believe that it was ok for boys to hit her. Within these formative early years, she learned to accept the abuse and keep quiet, or there would be repercussions. In keeping silent, she allowed herself to be in many abusive and toxic relationships throughout most of her life. This misguided mindset led to a life of rebellion. She turned to drugs and alcohol and left home at 13, eventually finding her way into a private group home for troubled teens. Now she knows her renegade attitude at the time was her cry for help.

Cheryl knew she was destined to be in the beauty industry when she was 11 years old, and she was not only painting her friends' and family's nails but her Doberman's nails as well.

The only school that taught Esthetics was 400 miles away in another Canadian province, and she was broke. She began selling stitchery at home parties to make enough money to pay for her schooling. After earning enough money to pay for her course, off to school she went, leaving her two children behind with her parents. Immersing herself day and night in her study, she was focused on completing her education quickly and getting back home to her kids. Cheryl's dedication paid off, graduating in half the scheduled time and with honors. Cheryl's parents were self-employed and hardworking; she claims this is where she learned her solid work ethic and started direct sales at 16.

Empowering Result

With her diploma in hand, she returned home with a huge mission. Her vision to open a local school would now provide the opportunity for a single mother to gain her education locally. She took a job and began developing what was needed to open the school. One and a half years later, at the age of 22, she opened the first Esthetics School in her province and has been an entrepreneur ever since. As her business grew, she continued to look to the future, educating thousands of students and participating in many exciting life changes for others.

Cheryl's known as the single mom who did – and the badass mom who still does, she never gives up on her dreams. She knows all too well the struggles of being a single mom, filling the role of both parents. Cheryl now coaches and encourages others to persevere through tough times, especially when they want to quit, and even quit life as she at times considered. That was not an option because two children depended on her. Their dad abandoned them at a very young age. She had no financial or physical support, so she often had to work two jobs – sometimes three. At times she was so broke and tired all she could do was cry and pray. No matter how exhausted she felt, it was still her sole responsibility to provide for her children and not show weakness.

Cheryl had to start over and rebuild from zero no less than ten times; through all these hardships and experiences, she has grown into the person she is today. She never gives up.

The importance of women's contributions

As a nurturing woman, Cheryl has helped to empower others by:

- Being an example to show that you can overcome your challenges.
- She worked with the less fortunate and street kids, encouraging them to overcome their circumstances to always be the best they can be.
- Accepting others exactly where they are in life, not judging and helping transform them to what they know deep inside they can become.

Cheryl still gets emotional when she tells the story of a student who had gotten out of prison and was on the streets, a single mom, broken and scared. Today this woman is in a fulfilling, stable, loving relationship with Mr. Wonderful; they have purchased a home. She runs her Esthetics business from there while contributing to society, and her son is now completing college.

Women perform exceptional services for the world. This is important because women are very empathic and compassionate, which the world needs. It is imperative for women to support each other, lift and encourage each other to strive for greatness. Women in leadership roles act as examples to other women and young girls who are becoming women.

Greatest Achievement

Here is another example of pushing through and never giving up. At 45 years of age, she was involved in a tragic motorcycle accident in the USA and had to stay there a month to recover. Wheelchair-bound for almost a year and in rehab therapy daily for years after. She could not maintain her largest location, and to her heartache, she was forced to close. Not being able to pay her bills, the landlord repossessed the building and all her equipment, including her personal belongings.

Cheryl was forced to be creative in order for her business to survive, and she developed a new way to educate her students. She made training videos at her kitchen table, which became DVDs and then completely online. This was the most outstanding achievement by becoming the first in North America (possibly the world) to offer classes through online education for Esthetics and Nail Technology. This new online school made her a pioneer in the industry while setting new standards and examples for others to follow. She remembers saying to a best friend... "If I only get one student a month, this will be great." This method took off, and by 2012 she had more students online than in the classroom, so she closed her locations and went 100% online. Her business expanded from the street corner to across the globe. Today, she has graduated thousands of students and is still excited about helping others grow and change their lives for the better.

She has Trademarked and branded her own line of Spa One nail and beauty products, has a full distribution center, founded several businesses, salons/spas, education centers, a podcast show, co-authored books, and holds copyrights on several training manuals.

Cheryl's greatest achievements:

Personally – overcoming every setback life threw at her, never quitting on her dream, and raising two amazing adult children who positively contribute to society.

Professionally, she found a need and filled it. She opened the first school of its kind in an area where there wasn't one. She then envisioned the possible demand for online education on a platform where anything other than hands-on was taboo – going against the grain and doing it anyway. It was an idea ten years ahead of its time. She struggled through, and it paid off now, having a global company educating people worldwide.

Additionally, starting a company to teach women self-care in the nail industry from home due to money restraints and COVID protocols. She has produced training videos and provides products to the at-home market.

An Inclusive and Diverse World

Here are five methods Cheryl has used to be inclusive while harnessing the power of diversity:

1. Mainly helping women by providing a new career to earn income for themselves and their families.
2. Flexibility in learning style – they can study part-time or full-time.
3. Geographically – the online platform allows them to study anytime, anywhere, and on any device.
4. Available for all gender and races – Male or Female and in any country, which allows their curriculum.

5. Affordable – payment plan and reduced rates compared to regular schools.

Strategies to Succeed in Our COVID Changed World

COVID-19 changed the world, but her vision of an online teaching platform was ahead of its time, and her company has risen in the face of a difficult situation. Cheryl's determination, innovative strategies, and forward-thinking led to her success. When all schools or any business with a personal touch were forced to shut down, her business flourished. They never lost a day of business and changed how beauty is taught forever. She had continuously struggled to prove this business model would be successful, and it is.

Author's Quote

Life is an endless beginning…. live with passion and purpose. by Cheryl Thibault

Bio

Cheryl Thibault is a visionary, entrepreneur, multi-business owner, educator, and game-changer in the beauty industry, focusing on healing, inspiring, and serving, providing hope and education to others.

The CEO and founder of TBO Ventures Inc., Spa One, and Mirage Spa Education Inc., the world's first online trade school. Cheryl has been creating and educating for 40 years. She actively integrates love, understanding, and compassion into all areas of her life as she influences thousands around the world to carry that forward.

These past few years, she has found herself on a new journey, a journey to find herself, to find the voice that was once silenced and use it. She now sees herself as a person of value, here to make a difference and does. All her tragedies are now her greatest stories which she is sharing, educating those who want education and uplifting those who need uplifting.

Known as THE SINGLE MOM WHO DID - and STILL DOES

Learn more about this author

Follow me on Facebook, Instagram, LinkedIn, and subscribe to my podcast The Walk Of Life.

Instagram = cherylthibault1

Linkedin.com/in/cherylthibault/

Facebook.com/cheryltbo

thewalkoflifestories.com - podcast

Free e-book and bonuses in my personal book Career in the Beauty Industry - Discover if it's for you. Including contributions to some of the biggest names in the beauty Industry. -

Chapter 12

Healthy Food, Healthy Life, Healthy Relationship

Vi Ho, DDS, MSD
The Ultimate Relationship Chef

Introduction

How many of you feel like your life is overwhelmed? How many feel like the opportunity for yourself is gone after having kids? How many feel like you have the burning desire to dig deeper and do more but don't know where to start? Dr. Vi can definitely raise her hand for all of the above.

She got to that point in her life where she answered yes to all of those questions. One day, tired of wondering, she decided to start doing it! Telling herself just start doing something, and along the way, her why, where, and how became clearer. Although she didn't know the answer initially, she knew that, at the very least, she needed to surround herself with those who inspired her. Don't be afraid to reach out, as some groups and individuals have burning desires to share and guide others to success. That's the faith you need to have to get you started and keep you going. Positivity is such an important piece of the puzzle and could impact you in many wonderful ways.

Mission

Dr. Vi's mission is to help people live a healthy life. Not just live a healthy life but also empower them to change themselves.

She offers education and tools to continue practicing a healthier lifestyle. She reinforces her knowledge through an educational program that will last a lifetime. She wants people to believe that their health is their wealth. She not only educates but offers a community for individuals that want to share their knowledge, practices, and recipes to live a healthy lifestyle. Dr. Vi walks her talk and talks her walk in her own practice.

Dr. Vi is a Root Canal Specialist. In her practice, every day, she strives to find ways to perform her job well in all aspects, such as how she delivers procedures to her patients. Dr. Vi intentionally considers healthy practices with respect to her client's whole body. The way she does one thing, she does all things. She is not just a Biological Root Canal Specialist but known as the ultimate relationship chef. Naturally, she loves her family dearly and wants to give them the best life possible by feeding their bodies and souls with healthy foods, a healthy lifestyle, and healthy relationships. The best tool she has to achieve all of the above, resulting in a HAPPIER LIFE, is COOKING. She hopes to share her experiences to help nourish and flourish the members of this community to achieve that happier and more meaningful life that they deserve!

Mission Statement: To help others use cooking as a tool to build healthier bodies and meaningful relationships simultaneously.

134

Vi's goal is to coach at minimum a handful of people to have this healthy way of life and live in a healthy body. It is about the enjoyment of cooking, not just feeding our body physically but also feeding our family in an environment while enjoying the dynamics of a community. Dr. Vi Ho thinks everything is all tied in together.

Vision

Dr. Vi believes a healthy diet typically includes nutrient-dense foods. She believes food is our medicine. She sees people cooking more nutritious meals that support the immune system, benefiting from her Ultimate Relationship Chef program. Her vision includes seeing people's self-esteem increase because cooking is an act of gaining patience and mindfulness. Cooking is an outlet for creative expression and a way of communicating your passions and serving those you love. Feed a belly and win their heart!

Vision Statement: To live in a world where everyone cooks and eats healthy immune-boosting food while building meaningful relationships.

Quote from a Visionary Leader

"My mission in life is not merely to survive but to thrive and to do so with some passion, some compassion, some humor, and some style." By Maya Angelou

Admiration of a Visionary Leader

- Determination: Got her to where she is today. She was determined to leave home at the age of 16 to find a new life for herself and did so successfully.
- Perseverance: if she didn't have this trait, she wouldn't have lasted and be where she is today.
- Connector: Believe your net worth is your network; She has many connections and loves connecting people.

Journey Of Discovering the Greatness Within

Vi's grandmother was a profound influence in her life. Grandmother grew up during the war in Vietnam, got married, and had four children. Unfortunately, her marriage ended with abuse and tyranny that left her a single mother with four children to care for. With no education, life became challenging. She had to leave each of her children in different places with different relatives to go to work to make ends meet. The pinnacle of it all was when she got burned in a gasoline fire at her retail gasoline business. Her grandmother was hospitalized for three months living in agony. She persevered and was devoted to her children and grandchildren through it all. The family was blessed with grandma's love, and she now follows that example in raising her family today.

Vi doesn't like to think that she had struggles, although many seem to see it that way. She feels like "struggles" are required to succeed and are just a part of life. She is very grateful to have encountered rough spots that helped her achieve a meaningful life today. She loves to help by passing on her pearls of knowledge to others and helping them embrace struggles and become more successful than she is.

Empowering Results

Nurturing others is her strength. Nurturing should be emotional and physical. To correctly identify what a person needs or best nurture them, we need first to listen and observe. There is no one-size-fits-all approach as we are unique in our own way. Vi has nurtured others emotionally by listening and identifying herself with their situation to give advice and motivational words that fit their needs. We need to remember it is not about us; it is about them and how we can help make them better! Her favorite way to nurture is through physical nurturing, through cooking, as she loves to cook. It is also her tool to make people feel loved and show that she cares about them without saying a word! To have a healthy mind, we need to have a healthy body. Eating well is crucial to having a healthy body. It is what keeps us going and able to last to enjoy the fruit of our labor.

Vi thinks a lot of times that we sabotage our own success. We limit ourselves, and fear is ultimately the main reason. Fear is a four-letter word that could significantly impact our success. When Dr. Vi or others need motivation, she reminds us that fear holds us back. We need to broaden our perspective and shift our minds to the end prize as this is very useful in removing fear. Often, 'women have a lot of self-doubts because we're such perfectionists, and we're so hard on ourselves.' When she is in this situation, she remembers her mother's words. "Just try your best. As long as your action is true and sincere, there should be no shame if there is a failure; just keep trying because no one is perfect."

God made two genders - men and women because each has different strengths and are unique. Women add value to the world; they are the mothers of the talented and successful people of the world! Women are not just wise; they are tough, resilient, and compassionate all in one. These feminine values help people become more well-rounded. Vi supports women first by speaking up for them whenever possible and then supporting and contributing their efforts. Lastly, just simply be there and listen to them when they need an ear to listen.

Dr. Vi Ho has a Facebook group called the Ultimate Relationship Chef. This group shares recipes and ways to cook and eat healthier, building relationships while you are at it.

Dr. Vi has a special place in her heart for helping others. Beyond helping people to eat healthily, she has assisted in other ways.

Dr. Vi has been influenced by western culture and her mother by Asian culture. These can be very different worlds. Dr. Vi's mother helps her siblings by sending money to them in Vietnam. They are not always as respectful and grateful as one would hope they would be. This results in her mom having hurt feelings. Through Dr. Vi's knowledge, she has been able to help her mother change her perspective. The change is in her mother's heart. Instead of a sense of duty, she now gives from the heart because it makes her feel good. Her heart is now happy, and she benefits from that. Her mom is much happier now and continues to give. How the receiver of the gifts feels is up to them.

Dr. Vi believes women perform exceptional service to the world and thinks it is essential because women offer services different from men. Women don't just offer exceptional services; they offer the nurturing emotional support to go along with the services. When women tie the emotional support with their services, they present a complete package. The service without the mental or the emotional aspect lacks the glue to hold it all together. This is similar to how the mother in a home nurtures the family and is the glue that holds the family unit together.

Both men and women work to provide for their families, but they do it differently and are equals but not equals. Neither gender is higher or lower; they bring different strengths and unique gifts to the table. Women feel and connect; they have the ability to nurture this is something most men cannot do.

When women discipline children, we try to understand the child coming from the emotional side, the mental aspect

138

we don't just 'matter of fact' with them as men do. Working things out from the mental aspect has greater results.

All great men were Born and Raised by great women, so at the end of the day, you can really see who the ultimate leader is.

Dr. Vi says the world would be very cut and dry if there were only men. The women bring in the support; they listen and say, I am listening, I understand, and share supportive words like, you've got this, and I am here for you.

She sees women as being very strong. Women can be a tower of strength with an ear to listen and a sincere voice to encourage.

Greatest Achievement

Dr. Vi's greatest achievement is providing her children with a complete family full of love with grandparents by their side 24/7. She realized her biggest goal in life has always been to find stability in finance and relationships within her immediate family. And she has done just that. She grew up so poor and vowed to find a better life for her family. To be able to take care of her parents, not let them worry about the daily expenses of life. To be able to say thank you for all their sacrifices with actions of being their financial support. Provide them with a family environment full of love and laughter where they can spend time with grandchildren and be a part of their lives. To have great mealtimes together every day. Dr. Vi can proudly say that she has provided all that, but it was not easy. It took a lot of planning, sacrifices, and intentions to make it happen, and it is all worthwhile.

An Inclusive and Diverse World

Dr. Vi Ho believes the five best practices on harnessing the power of diversity and inclusion for innovation are establishing a sense of belonging for everyone, empathic leadership, maximizing joy, connection with others, minimizing fear, and focusing on individual thriving.

Establishing a sense of belonging for everyone is the first and one of the most crucial practices. When people feel they belong, they are more willing to open up and contribute.

Second, empathic leadership is required to be an effective leader. Empathy allows leaders to identify with different feelings, feel them within themselves, and show that they genuinely care. Once the process has started, maximizing joy and connection are needed to keep it going.

Fourth, we must remember not to lead with fear. Fear will create distrust, narrow perspectives, and overturn inclusion to exclusion.

Fifth and last, focusing on individuals will help each person maximize their potential. Together, we will have one powerful force.

Strategies to Succeed in Our COVID Changed World

When COVID happened and brought along the panic, Dr. Vi told herself first and foremost, be calm! Nothing lasts forever, even the worst of situations reminding herself that every cloud has a silver lining. Even the worst situations have some positive aspects; you just have to be open to it and look for it. Remember, one of the great things about being human is we can adapt. While others panicked about their business, Dr. Vi looked at ways to change so that her business would stay afloat and be more efficient. The silver lining received from this event regarding her business was that she was able to change her work schedule and patient appointments with great results, becoming more profitable, working less, and having more time with her family. On the personal aspect, the COVID-19 event brought her closer to the reality that relationships and life are super fragile. It is not just death itself that can separate people. Catastrophic events like this can separate and leave us with sadness worse than death because we are aware. Still, we cannot do anything about it. Dr. Vi became determined to have more intentions in living a better work and home life. Without determination, we don't have the drive, and without the drive, we won't have results.

Author's Quote

Your healthy cooking is like your bank account. Your wealth is your health. Dr. Vi Ho

Bio

Dr. Vi Ho was born in Viet Nam and immigrated to America with her family at the age of eight. They arrived as poor immigrants with only $ 50 in their pocket. Her parents had to work long hours to provide for us and our family back in Viet Nam. Because of this hardship, she was determined to fight for a better future and obtained her undergraduate degree in Biology at Texas A&M University on a full scholarship. She then received immediate acceptance to dental school. She finished her Doctor of Dental Surgery degree Suma Cum Laude at Creighton University in Omaha, Nebraska. Her lucky streak brought her straight into a three-year endodontic program which only two residents are accepted per year. Happily, with Vi's determined attitude, she obtained her endodontic specialist certification and master's degree in Science of Dentistry at the University of Texas at Houston.

Learn more about this author

Join the Ultimate Relationship Chef Facebook Group Community

https://www.facebook.com/groups/584143215530184/

ELEVATING AS A GLOBAL VISIONARY LEADER

Chapter 13

Standing in Your Power, Walking in Your Greatest and Leading with Authenticity

H.E. Desziree Richardson, DLA, DLITT
Founder of Women of Heart Awards (WOHA),
Face of WOHA, & Gentlemen of Heart Awards (GOHA)

Introduction

Dr. Desziree Richardson, DLA, DLITT is a thought leader, transformation and motivational speaker, International best-selling author, model, humanitarian, and entrepreneur. Although she is a solid businesswoman, she feels a genuine desire and devotion to the well-being and welfare of her fellow human beings. She enjoys being a service to others. Dr. Desziree believes her sole purpose in sharing her story and wisdom is to help empower positive changes in the lives of many people around the world.

Mission

Dr. Desziree uses her experiences and voice as a vehicle and an instrument calling for change. To empower, heal, motivate, and help transform lives into those filled with love, kindness, peace, abundance, and acceptance. She has purposely designed creative projects for women's empowerment, passion, and soul purpose. Her platforms bring a powerful magnetic energy and a unique array of women advancement projects to celebrate, motivate and empower women worldwide.

Mission Statement: Dr. Desziree's mission is to help change lives and positively influence others through her empowering projects. Her wish is for every to be happy and to feel inclusive.

To live in a world where peace, love, kindness, and the energy of cosmic love can be radiated and felt through every human existence and experience.

Vision

She envisions a world of hope far from the perils of the ego to replace the elements with compassion, kindness, peace, and tolerance.

"Success is not about the money you are making but the difference you are making in people's lives."

Michelle Obama

Dr. Desziree greatly admires Michelle Obama as a Visionary Leader who is the pride of hope and inspiration for countless women across the globe. She is admired for her loyalty, integrity, strength, charisma, dedication, relentlessness, wisdom, voice, leadership, and compassion.

Mrs. Obama's characteristics and courageous attributes bring about a positive change in our mindset around the globe and her family. She is becoming an icon of positivity by breaking the barriers of limitation. She is challenging the status quo of racism and doubts by replacing these elements with inspiration for women of color to rise to the occasion of greatness.

Journey of Discovering the Greatness Within

Dr. Desziree took counsel with her universal inner voice. The law of attraction drove her to pursue her dreams of controlling her destiny and improving her three children's livelihood. In 2008 she headed to the United Kingdom with her children to pursue a media degree and career. Despite the moments of self-doubt, obstacles, dark clouds, and poor judgment, she pushed onward. This dream encapsulated her history and the fears that sometimes cast a dark shadow over her present and future. She believes with the right guide; she will overcome the self-sabotage that has dogged her for years. 2020 and 2021 have been challenging years for all of us. As a single parent at home, raising three young kids, working, studying, teaching, and setting up and managing her online businesses were some of the significant challenges. Experience had given her the strength to overcome the difficulties she had no control over. The creator has played an essential constructive role in her life with the many challenges she faced and resolved. However, she can still witness the full power as the icy hand of fear, particularly fear of success, draws her back.

Dr. Desziree has managed to resolve her challenges while others tenuously linger in theirs. She realized she had to venture into the world and find a new place to become the person she was meant to be. Then allowing the universe to recognize her talents and reconcile her inner world with her inner potential. She launched a few brands, including www.womenoffoundation.com, www.happymoodswagger.com, www.uptopswag.com, and www.faceofwoha.com.

The Women of Heart Foundation's launch was achievable because of her heart's desire to help many people in need. This is a not-for-profit, charitable organization based in the UK and working worldwide, which is established to support women and children in various focused ways. Specifically, they inspire people to get involved and volunteer. They also promote, educate, empower, and raise funds for women and children in the UK and underprivileged remote countries worldwide.

One of their main objectives at Women of Heart Foundation is to help people advance in life, and they have a particular focus on those individuals who are excluded from the best opportunities through youth, old age, illness, disability, or through challenging socio-economic circumstances.

The Women of Heart Foundation provides community support, custom events, and programs. Dr. Desziree's programs and events focus on physical, educational, recreational, and leisure time activities to improve people's lives developing their skills, capacities, and capabilities. These projects aim to enable everyone to participate in society as mature and responsible individuals. Women of Heart celebrate successful women in various aspects of their deeply rooted beauty. Dr. Desziree's platform brought awareness to the beauty of diversity, the power of words, and messaging. Fulfilled women worldwide experienced an incredible journey of sharing enlightenment and empowerment.

Empowering Results

Dr. Desziree's platforms not only recognize women who are changing the world by fighting and bringing positive changes through their work. They are preparing the next generation of female leaders. In 2020, they ran a successful campaign with the face of WOHA diversity awareness leaders.

Through the Face of WOHA, we give a voice to those who have the potential to become leaders and icons. However, the work provides more worthy causes and opportunities for women to work with.

Diversity is also an issue that has been overlooked. As a leader, she is determined to bring positive changes in the world through these platforms to help women find their voices, celebrate their achievements, and spread diversity awareness. There is a future for every little girl to have the chance to chase their dreams and realize them. Voices of women won't be lost in the crowd. Their achievements and capabilities will be celebrated. Stories of their journey, struggles, and success will inspire others to do better and achieve whatever they want.

If there is a story or a vision you are connecting to, and you hope it will make a difference, please get involved with organizations. Volunteering in your communities has helped Dr. Desziree learn transferable skills for business, career, and job prospects. She is sure you will adopt different skills to help you expand as you get involved. She had the opportunity to meet amazing people along the journey involved in community development and humanitarian work. She encourages you to show up and show a substantial amount of interest to learn. You can learn the necessary skills to elevate you, prepare and propel you in the right direction to receive unexpected opportunities.

Clarisa Romero Face of WOHA

Furthermore, writing a book to share your story and share your expertise and experiences will also open doors for your message to be shared and listened to by millions. You will need to have a positive and creative mindset for wisdom and understanding, strength, and determination to initiate the legacy you plan to leave in the world. It would be best to be empowered with crucial elements of everyday living, such as self-determination, self-love, self-esteem, self-confidence, self-reliance, self-care, and self-love. Show them compassion and teach them to be kind, grateful, humble, and caring.

You are here for a reason, and for whatever that reason is, it is your destiny from birth. Once you find your true calling and purpose, it allows you freedom. Still, that freedom comes with taking full responsibility for your actions with great intentions for yourself and society. With your destiny path before you, Dr. Desziree asks you to do one thing and put it into everything you do; it is called love, and it is free. If we all do this, the world will heal.

It is helpful to be prepared and start making the changes you need to create your future and legacy. Start by surrounding yourself with ambitious people. The way you live your life will become more important to you.

 Dr. Desziree encourages you to start believing that you deserve, and it is possible to achieve what your heart desires. She inspires women to become innovative by creating ideas to help them succeed by doing what they love and enjoy. She encourages them to have good intentions for the world and recommends that they remain grateful and humble during each step they take on their journey.

She encourages other women to make a positive difference in the world. She will use her platforms to motivate others to believe in the power of choice. Each of us can choose what we allow to manifest in our lives;

opportunities could open for them with the right decisions. Moreover, remember to thank everyone who played an essential role in helping you reach your full potential. When you are at the top, please help others; it is vital to give back. You were created in the world to love and be kind.

Dr. Desziree uses her voice and leadership skills to empower children as Mother Nature during the International Educational Handshake at London Metropolitan University. She created and hosted the Women Involvement Charity Concert at the University of West London, which raised Funds for Future Sense Charity.

As a Project Leader at the University of West London, Dr. Desziree led and organized projects, volunteers, and events in the community, such as planting trees in Gunnersbury Park and creating outdoor community projects that benefit the community environment. She has also helped with fundraising for the Have A Heart Appeal, Help a London Child, The Classic Foundation, campaigning for the Hunger Summit, IF Enough Food for Everyone, and UNICEF.

Dr. Desziree believes women are the guiding lights in our rational world. Throughout the universe, women are the pillars of our hospitals, schools, care infrastructure, and in our homes. They are also the managers in our offices, the dreamers in our creative world, leaders in our communities, and the beating hearts of our humanitarian sectors. They are the fixers, careers, teachers, leaders, and peacemakers. In all these spheres, women's light is central and undiminished. Through empowering platforms such as the Women of Heart Awards, she supports women. WOHA is a great forum to forge connections between like-minded women. The WOHA network of leaders teaches and supports women on empowering themselves from within. The organization helps others find their voice to become leaders and decision-makers through the stories they share. The is work geared towards promoting excellence, generosity, and pride in women's actions. We enjoy acknowledging and celebrating their achievements.

Greatest Achievement

She has contributed to many funds and awareness-raising campaigns, including live auction bids with other celebrities and volunteering at a UNICEF Children's Champion. She's received awards and recognition for her work, including the England Gold Award, reflecting her passion, leadership, and dedication.

She is The Women of Heart Foundation (WOHA) founder launched in 2020. The WOHA is a platform designed to connect, support, and promote women to become instrumental leaders making the world a better place by clicking diverse women for a better cause. The WOHA raises funds to empower and educate women globally, honoring fifty iconic global women who make a difference in the world.

An Inclusive and Diverse World

Diversity and inclusion are essential in a world that is shifting swiftly. However, as humans, we should all gather our good thoughts and deeds by accepting and welcoming different cultures and religions in the workplace, society, and social norms. Furthermore, gender diversity can help individuals thrive in innovation and investment. A diverse and inclusive team of leaders and their characteristics is unique. They depict vast amounts of opinions and views that are relevantly essential and improve the quality of the workplace in terms of transparency and tolerance. Dr. Desziree as a visionary leader, her projects sustain, support, and implement diversity and inclusion. The face of WOHA represents a sense of belonging and a contribution to embracing these factors. The aim is to connect diversity for a better cause, create awareness, and invite women worldwide to showcase a healthy, balanced world and share messages. Messages that will help change the world positively while showcasing the beauty in diverse women as a visual component.

She wishes everyone to feel included and live happily in a world that accepts diversity and inner peace while enjoying the radiating cosmic love's energy. Moreover, let us continue to speak, feel, and spread love through our thoughts and actions with love and gratitude.

Strategies To Succeed in Our COVID Changed World

During COVID-19 lock-down, she incorporated the following tools: believing and trusting in the process with gratitude, prayer, and inspiring creativity. These all helped her overcome the self-sabotage that has dogged her for years. 2020 /21 were challenging years for all of us. As a single parent at home, raising three young kids, working, studying, homeschooling, and setting up and managing her online businesses were some of her significant challenges.

Her experience had given her the strength to overcome the obstacles she had no control over. She believes the creator played an essential constructive role in her life as she moved beyond a host of challenges she was facing and resolving. However, she can still witness the full power as the icy hand of fear, particularly fear of success, draws her back. Dr. Desziree took counsel with her universal inner voice. The law of attraction drove her to pursue her dreams. She wanted to control her destiny and improve her three children's livelihood. She wants to reach a broader audience, gain credibility, impact the lives of every human in existence, and create a positive change in the minds of readers, listeners, and viewers, changing the world through changing lives, empowering the world to become kinder and to share love towards humanity through her projects.

Moreover, she has managed to resolve some issues while others tenuously linger. She realized that she had to venture into the world and find a new place to become the person she was meant to be. She allowed the universe to recognize her talents and reconcile her inner world with her potential. During COVID, she launched a few brands, including www.womenofheartawards.com, www.happymoodswagger.com, www.uptopswag.com, and www.faceofwoha.com.

Author's Quote

Her motto is to Break the Ice, empower better working relationships among women and advocate for positive healing with love and support on the planet.

"There is great joy in the universe, but you have to find yourself and create your inner pleasure to reap the beauty of it. There is only one you. Be you. The world needs you in all your glory. Put love in all you do; when love wins, the world wins."

Bio

Dr. Desziree's authentic presence and sincere transparency have showcased her unique talents as a speaker, author, media personality, broadcaster, and witty reporter. She writes high-quality fiction and nonfiction. She has swiftly become an international bestselling author with a dedicated fan base and successfully moved into the world of international publishing. She is sincere, personable, and a consummate professional. Her magnetic voice made her famous with her listening audience as one-part smooth, two parts delightful, and a large portion of entertaining and joyful communication. Alongside her established media and celebrity career, Dr. Desziree is dedicated to helping people in need and has a real passion for empowering women, volunteering, and philanthropy.

Learn more about this author

VISIT	www.desziree.com
	@desziree00
	https://www.facebook.com/FollowDesziree
	www.instagram.com/desziree?=nametag

Chapter 14

Leader, Entrepreneur, Connector, Educator

Nontsikelelo 'Ntsiki' Ncoco

Transformational Leadership Requires Integrity

Introduction

Ntsiki is a management consultant with more than 30 years of experience within human resource services.

Corporations hire Ntsiki Ncoco to assist in training and coaching their managers to become incredible leaders. Not just leaders who hold positions of power but those who acknowledge and exercise power to lead with integrity. Ntsiki consults in the corporate environment where integrity and authenticity should be displayed and maintained in daily operations. She leads with integrity showing her client's managers and leaders better approaches to succeed with their staff, leading to business success. The bottom line is businesses reach their ultimate potential by reaching their goals and vision of their strategic plans.

Through hard work and determination, she gained visibility in the marketplace by networking, sharing referrals, and finding the right partners to collaborate with locally and internationally. She sponsors and moderates business summits and hosts different guests and keynote speakers to empower entrepreneurs. She is a motivational public speaker and a masterclass facilitator.

Entrepreneurial experience has taught Ntsiki assertiveness, resilience, and determination to grow her business, lead others to do the same, and become a preferred service provider.

Mission Statement: To empower leaders through education to lead with competence and integrity.

Ntsiki Ncoco believes she can change the narrative by empowering others through coaching and providing a knowledge base for leaders to be empowered and grow from mediocrity into greatness.

Vision

Ntsiki will continue to raise awareness through training and empowering leaders. She hosts business leadership summits as a moderator, sponsor, and keynote speaker to expand potential. Inspiring future leaders and her influence positively impacting all levels of leadership in the workplace, communities, and church with the goal to excel in their roles.

With a goal to provide businesses the tools required for economic growth, she has been partnering with the WWCA organization and identifying relevant guests to speak at her hosted business summits, where she empowers entrepreneurs.

Vision Statement: To advance outstanding leadership and social justice, inspire global leaders to pass on the leadership baton, and leave a legacy of generations that will lead with integrity.

"To those who oppose us, we say, Strike the woman, and you strike the rock." - Winnie Mandela, 1966

Admiration of a Visionary Leader

PUBLIC SECTOR
LEADER
OF THE YEAR
Tsakani Maluleke

Pic caption: Tsakani Maluleke, Auditor General, South Africa

Ms. Tsakani Maluleke, Auditor General, South Africa, continues to make history as the first woman to occupy a senior position in the office of the auditor-general, South Africa. The South African President appointed her for a seven-year non-renewable term, taking effect from December 1, 2020. Tsakani Maluleke is the Public Servant of the Year for 2021.

Ms. Maluleke's humbleness, assertiveness, resilience, and clarity of her clean audit leadership role on how to serve the country is inspiring. She is a focused Visionary Leader with a great professional record in the country's governance and executive leadership. She is the supporter who honored the launch of Power to Lead with Integrity Foundation with her expertise, alongside six great speakers.

Ntsiki admires her leadership style with an ability to raise the bar, being the first African woman to hold the position in the country. She exhibited a sustained endowment of ethics, authenticity, resilience, and determination.

She aligned with leading with distinct and uprightness to advance the leadership governance in Africa. Running her business taught her resilience and determination to be the order of the day in growing the operations with success.

Journey of Discovering the Greatness Within

Pic caption: Ntsiki Ncoco's Awards & Acknowledgements

Knowing who you are, why you have been uniquely designed with your fingerprints and your values that no one else on earth has a duplicate.

"Passion is the greatness born within you, small as a mustard seed, water it daily with love in action to grow and bless the world around you." Ntsiki Ncoco

Ntsiki grew up using writing and drawing to express her inspired thoughts into context, capturing them for good use. Journaling her feelings was her way of self-talk and how she wished to be heard. She would write poems when triggered by a personal feeling or experience. This allowed her to express her feelings on paper, put a title, and align the poem with an adventure.

She desired a career in the fashion industry, but things did not unfold in that direction. Ntsiki found educational psychology and economics courses resonated with her, and she followed this path for her university studies. At the honors level in Education, Curriculum Studies was a requirement. She loved the flow of the specific learning standards and the content used to organize and teach courses. She imagined herself beyond the classroom and often had visions of herself standing in front of several people conducting training sessions and delivering a speech. She developed a love for Trade Economics with its study of the structure of international financial interactions. With the investigation of trades, she decidedly chose Economics as a major. Later in Management Consulting, the visions from her earlier life became real.

Ntsiki has taken her formal education and skills combined with her passion for successfully building collaborations with other global organizations. These collaborations are with businesses and projects in the trades and education sectors, including three universities. The goal is to establish an entrepreneurship skills development academy for economic growth and commodity trades with business linkages. Ntsiki is an eZWayNetwork Affiliate International Ambassador and has recently been booked as a Podcast Guest, by three radio stations, Hosted by Hollywood Award Winners.

[Peace, Love and Bring a Bat, The Perfect Zone, and Hollywood Red Carpet Radio Show by Hollywood Awards Winners.]

Pic caption: Ntsiki Ncoco: eZWay Affiliate International Ambassador

She was passionate about conducting workshops and seminars in the workplace, communities, and churches. Coupled with public speaking, she discovered her clear purpose. With her purpose acknowledged, she focused with great success on knowing how to pitch while negotiating deals. She states that it is an absolute joy and pleasure to prepare her presentations for any appointment. She is a creative content writer who inspires others. She confesses that her articles must first inspire her, then she creates the content. Ntsiki has edited a few published books and articles with a critical eye of what a reader should enjoy and find inspiring when reading. She ends by citing that she never looks down on her humble beginnings. Her first formal job was as a Typist at Walter Sisulu University, where she worked during the day and studied as a part-time student at night after work.

Life can be tough and unfair; out of the pains of the past, a character is developed. Held at gunpoint during a house robbery was a traumatic event. Ntsiki later faced what looked like the ultimate challenge as she was falsely accused and taken to the Supreme Court of Law. These and other experiences of hardships can have a lasting effect as she still has flashbacks.

In these unexpected inhuman tragedies, she says as a believer to the Almighty God, her Creator, her automatic first step is to call upon this higher power. God was the only power she believed in and trusted to come to her rescue.

Her unwavering faith and belief in the power of prayer was the only tool to help her go through these challenges. Without a doubt, Ntsiki, the daughter of the one she calls 'Abba Father,' delivered her from those adversities and healed her, and she has forgiven the perpetrators. She says it was not easy but possible through the help of the power of God as her Counselor. She is forever grateful for the support and prayers of her friends, family, and church members.

These experiences, amongst others of struggling in the marketplace with no business and no income, have taught her resilience, determination, never quitting, and never to lose hope for a better tomorrow. She emphasizes that when coaching, mentoring, counseling, motivating, inspiring, praying for others and with them, she speaks from a point and position of knowing and having experienced all kinds of pain, emotionally, mentally, physically, and financially,

As you think about it, you become it; it is all in the state of your mind.

Positive Mindset:

All the steps one will take to scale through difficult times start in the mind. The thoughts must remain positive and focus on the prize.

Believe:

The biggest gift you can give to your legacy in your lifetime adventure is to believe in yourself.

Clarity with Focus:

Be clear 'why' you do what you do as your daily focus, revisit and affirm your goals and niche.

Beyond the challenges, stay focused on the cause.

Integrity:

Maintaining your integrity and staying true to yourself brings peace through every phase of the difficult changes and uncertainties as you fight forward.

Gratitude:

Being grateful for being alive and living in the moment prepares one for the next better level of living.

Elite leadership is born out of many learning curves. Being resilient is the superpower, which is the strength from within to sustain a mortal being.

Empowering Results

Ntsiki has a big heart and lives a life that includes loving the unlovable. She has learned to be patient with irritating personalities, forgiving others who have wronged her and treated her badly in the community and the workplace. She is open to embracing selfish personalities to share information or sponsor and support others to grow. The calm and grounded personality can focus on the road to success so not to be distracted on the way to your destiny.

Outcomes: Healing from the hurts of the past, distressing and offloading the unnecessary stress, building a strong character, determined to achieve goals beyond any negativity. Releasing women to speak up and have their voices heard for who they are. Peace and a positive mindset equals success.

To be Super Successful: Have your Vision and Mission written down, and work on it every day. Take Personality Assessment Tests; know who you are and identify your high and low values. Know your abilities & capabilities, know how you are designed, and have an action plan that speaks to your unique personality, character, passion, and purpose. Stay and focus on your lane of abilities. Never copy and paste someone's action plan. Never compete with anybody; only compete with your vision to achieve it and step closer to it every day. Live a life of peace and integrity and honor your life with a decent character to empower and inspire others even with indirect coaching. They will see your impact in your communities and your workplace. As you rise, lift others up with you. Be opened to learning from others, and share information to enrich others.

Keep empowering yourself with up-skilling in education; there are many free courses online for all disciplines. There is no excuse not to learn a new skill and be empowered. We shall overcome to lead the world through education. Ntsiki uses Nelson Mandela's great quotes on education: "Education is the great engine of personal development. Through education, the daughter of a peasant can become a doctor, the son of a mineworker can become the head of the mine, and a child of farmworkers can become the President of a great nation. It is what we make out of what we have, not what we are given, that separates one person from another."

"Education is the most powerful weapon which you can use to change the world."

Your Why? Is your legacy. Many influential global leaders had no degrees but were highly skilled with great life values. They were full of charisma yet not formally educated. Their legacy is in the books and museums. The combination is highly important in our era, and we have many informal and formal learning opportunities.

Pic caption: Ntsiki Ncoco with Amanda Matshaka, Founder of South African Heroes Awards.

Ntsiki has empowered, inspired, and trained executives who are both mature and youth leaders in the workplace, communities, and church to lead with integrity. She has been a Conference Speaker in different Women's Events and has spoken on various women's leadership topics.

Radio guest on three Radio Stations conducting Leadership Programmes.

Power to Lead with Integrity Foundation impact: Won a 2nd Runner Up on South African Heroes Awards 2020, Business Leadership Category. She was the Keynote Speaker at the South African Heroes Awards on July 18, 2020, Mandela Day. Mentoring and Coaching Youth & Executives to Create Content and Write to promote their Branding weekly on the Inspirer World -LinkedInItToWinIt platform. She motivates as an expert on weekly seminars.

She continues creating awareness for Women & Young Women to be aware of the WWCA Organization to join as members and make a global impact.

The Importance of Women's Contributions

Women are natural incubators of life and multipliers of greatness, a life channel to this earth, nurturers, educators, and heroines who understand all personalities and characters.

Women's power to lead with integrity must never be underestimated or their worth diminished. They are very good at leadership and decision-making. They are designed in unique ways to use their natural unique values and fingerprints wisely to expand a little idea into greater heights. Women make sure the whole village is fed from one garden. They share the little they have, support each other, and lift up their communities and society. No one will go hungry or uneducated where 'Women of Integrity' exist.

Women fight together for their 'right' rights to live in dignity and fairness for all. They turn their passion into purpose. W.O.M.A.N. are Warriors, Oasis, Magnanimous, Audacious, Nurturers; they are educators, best coaches, and mentors at any level in life.

Women love to share the knowledge they have gained, empower each other through education and grow together. Women leave a mark by their social services for all.

She Educates, Inspires, and Motivates Women in Leadership Modules presented through Workshops, Seminars, Coaching & Mentorship Sessions. Conference Speaking and attending other women's events, subscribing to Women's Forums, and collaborating with other women globally. Teach them to know their abilities and capabilities that we are all special, we have to leave our own legacies of integrity for the next generations. Forward with the spirit of Ubuntu.

Greatest Achievement

To be appointed to the Steering Committee and a lecturer at World Academy Clubs (WAC). This 'InterMan Startup' in knowledge for an online university based in Germany (supported by Technical University of Dresden) was initiated in March 2021. It is composed of international professors, scientists, experts, and students running educational programs and joint research work as a modern remote university based on online video conference communications supported with modern social media and mixed reality tools. Access to more than 2000 international professors and experts in different fields, covering all industries, is her greatest achievement being part of the global narrative changers from Africa.

An Inclusive and Diverse World

Diversity & Inclusion:

1. Establish a sense of belonging for everyone.

Building a brand means, including everyone from all walks of life, with skills to contribute to achieving the organization's goals with self-belonging to the environment. People act at their best once they feel comfortable and accepted by the teams and the organization. It is important to feel a sense of belonging, relax and have a home and family in the workplace; that is where you spend most of your time. Connect with the team and the organization, feel right then emotionally and psychologically free to perform at your best.

2. Execute Empathetic leadership.

Having a people-first strategy in an organization is a winning strategy. Serve its customers and fulfill the expectations of the shareholders and stakeholders. People need to be treated as they deserve; they bring diverse knowledge to solve the problems of the organization to achieve its goals.

3. Ongoing embraces of the culture of diversity.

A workplace is constantly changing, with short-term, medium-term, and long-term goals. Individuals sometimes have to measure daily the operations and practices. It can be through talks and team conversations. It helps the individual feel at ease, with honest support, advancing people to grow in different ways. All their new changes and habitual behaviors need guidance to be entwined for the good.

4. 360% leadership.

Leadership from the top-down is not an adequate best practice.

A winning strategy needs a top-down, bottom-up leadership style. A practice of different leadership styles makes its employees included as part of the strategy to succeed in the organization's goals with energetic, happy hearts.

5. Help individuals thrive without fear.

Fear can be a great motivator for people to perform to their best level. But on another note, fear can disarm people, lead them to distraction and resist leadership. It is automatic that people react differently to fear; it can bring different perspectives altogether. People are wired differently. When people are given an opportunity to be free to express their perspectives, inform, and set up conversations to narrate their stories, it gives them a sense of belonging with the flexibility to change as they feel honored being part of the game.

Strategies to Succeed in Our COVID Changed World

Throughout COVID, Ntsiki continued learning. Courses she completed include Health Healing Techniques, Physical Exercise Techniques, Mind Power, Personality Type Assessment for Executive Leadership, Contribution

Compass, Design Thinking, Personality Assessment, The Incredible You Coaching. ICT Integration Tools. Developed a Change Management Module. Published Articles on Uncertainty Management.

Also, Training for Board Directorship, with a company that finds jobs for women in Board positions.

Determination is important for success because it keeps one focused on the vision and mission you carry and believe in beyond any obstacles and challenges you are faced with. It sets one's mind to focus on positive thinking and possibilities. It is the driving force that gives the mind the ability to create solutions out of the box, with design thinking and advanced thinking to find a way to resolve any problem one is faced with and see it as a challenge to be resolved. It internally structures one's mindset to see the results beyond any failure and setbacks. It creates imaginations of what you want to achieve. You see it before it manifests in reality. It keeps checks and balances of the Mission and Vision you have for the mark you want to live on earth. It propels the great road to fulfill your destiny and inspire the world we live in. It is why you wake up and empower others and motivate them to achieve their greatness. It molds the character to stay in tune with the objectives of living a legacy of integrity and social justice for all. It makes great leaders out of any environment or background; it sees no failure nor giving up on a mission to focus on the prize. It propels one's energy to the greater ability to achieve ultimate capabilities through skills & enhance it with education.

Author's quote

"Power of Networking is the great give and get seed to your positive wealth of relationships and knowledge. It's a treasury that offers one a global virtual citizenship and influence."- Ntsiki Ncoco

Bio

A Management Consultant with more than 30 years of experience in HR Solutions. Ntsiki Ncoco is the Founder of Power To Lead With Integrity Inc & the Foundation. She has vast experience in Higher Institution Executive Management from the University of Transkei to UNISA / SA University's Vice Chancellor's Association.

eZWay Affiliate International Ambassador

Management Consultant at Power to Lead with Integrity Inc.

Focusing on Leadership Growth & Advancement; Human Resources Solutions.

Coaching and Mentoring of Women for Board Directorship with Global Chairwomen. Headhunting and Placements of women in Board Director positions.

Chairperson: CEO Clubs Worldwide SA Chapter and B2B Global Linkages.

Board Director of 5 organizations. (3 global and 2 locals.)

Learn more about this author

Offer link Article below

How To Personally Navigate Successfully During Change & Uncertainty by Ntsiki Ncoco

Follow Ntsiki Ncoco

https://ntsikincoco.com

https//linktr.ee/NtsikiNcoco

Chapter 15

Elevating Global Visionaries and Thought Leaders
Revolutionizing the Future of Women's Health

Helen Argyrou
Founder of Women of Truth

Introduction

Helen has a special talent for merging science with spirituality. She can spot the unique original selling point in a leader or speaker and their special message for the world. She helps coach leaders and speakers to become pioneering paradigm shifters. Her ability to integrate science and spirituality leads to articulating higher dreams and possible solutions for global issues with their knowledge and expertise. She then elevates them onto her world stages with her diverse European and global contacts. Global female leaders present their thought leadership on her unique WOMEN OF TRUTH platform and in her divine feminine leadership retreats in Cyprus.

A year before obtaining her degree in clinical psychology, she worked with rape survivors in South Africa, where a rape happens every 4 seconds. This work was challenging and heart-wrenching, which ultimately shaped her commitment to do something about gender-based violence in her professional work.

"(Helen is) A woman of magical, intuitive connection. If you haven't worked with her yet, ITS TIME". Dr. Eline Pedersen DC

Mission

Helen inspires, facilitates, and trains individuals, families, and leaders to self-actualize in coaching, mentoring, and visibility strategies that peak their performance. Her WOMEN OF TRUTH Conferences elevate global female leaders and speakers, revolutionizing health. They merge science with spirituality, tackling the psychoeducational piece that helps women elevate their understanding of integrative and holistic health. This includes the inherent repercussions of sexual abuse trauma and body-mind integration.

Helen welcoming one of her 160 WOMEN OF TRUTH Speakers to date, Dr. Smriti Dutta, Project development & management engineering specialist in Rotterdam.

Mission Statement: Elevate female Global Visionaries Leaders and spiritual feminism for greater impact on global issues.

Vision Statement

Elevate Global Visionaries female leaders and spiritual feminism for greater impact on global issues.

"Occasionally, we will be overwhelmed, but mostly we will be enchanted." Dr. Jean Houston

Admiration Of a Visionary Leader

Helen has always admired Dr. Jean Houston, an anthropologist, and teacher of mysticism, for her depth of knowledge, creative mind, and spirituality.

Depth of Knowledge - When Helen discovered she loved drumming and learned about the effects of rhythm on regulating the brain, she learned it is a scientific principle called entrainment. When a certain topic interest her, she tends to do a deep dive research into it. She has always appreciated personal experience and passion for a topic that is steeped with a deep study of it.

Deep study is important to her, so when she became fascinated with her passion for Drumming, she built a new website to share the information. She added all she could find on the science behind rhythm and its effect on the brain and consciousness. This led her to teachers and brilliant rhythmic wisdom that took her to the source of creation—the primordial pulse of the universe itself, an expression of vibration. Later she built the brand AhaIntelligence. Her fusion website Helen A.H.A. is based on a deep study of the pineal gland and powers of vision using imaginative brain procedures on the neuroscientific level. She found neurogenesis, neuroagility and cornerstoned them in her work, designed especially for the new leaders in a post COVID world.

Deep knowledge is something she pursues and loves; it is informative, and she relates it to the women's work she has been diving deep into. She became transfixed on investigating the real stories, reason, and breakthrough points for women to access their personal power and what she's come to call 'The politics of Identity.'

It was because of her study of the subject - from interviewing drag queens in South Africa for her masters' thesis at university; feminism, female leadership, to gender bias and later divine femininity that led her once again to question the deeper truth in it all. Recently, Helen interviewed 100 women to understand further the deeper truth about divine female leadership for changing times. She wrote a book about this research that reveals the missing link in gender inequality debates and why women still struggle collectively. The conclusions are both spiritual and profound.

You see, your deep knowledge can only be such if it is somehow also carrying some sense of wisdom. The Greeks called it 'gnosis,' which has inherently some version of universal truth. Evidencing that with proof, it is like all these women sharing the journeys they made reveals the path of wisdom. A guide for us all to remove the blinders we have and propagated in our daughters and sons. One that finally helps us all become the truth - not some political, personal, or psychologically defended illusion about reality. Deep Knowledge cultivates a path to freedom, freedom from myth, bias, and skewed perception.

Creative - Creativity is a conduit to higher realms of integration and inspiration. She uses it a lot to stay sane and to express her vision, upon which she then manifests that vision into reality.

The innovation and ingenuity of her life and work have evolved mainly due to her creative play in the world. It has become a primary way she expresses herself. Her creativity helps her in so many instances. Justina Pluktaite, who evaluated her dynamic leadership 360 review for Toastmaster speaker certification, said she solves problems creatively. As a leader, that's how she expands herself and her business, as it has led her to new areas and unique assimilations of knowledge, products, and services. Such as the original Aphrodite-based Leadership retreats that are a creative expression of the Feminine Divine.

The ancient priestess's legacy - playing the most ancient frame drum - used primordial sounds to emulate the rhythmic wisdom of the universe and Feminine Divine Mysteries in Cyprus

Spiritual - Understanding the deeper layers of our existence and how they have been understood and explained in various spiritual principles is forever important to her. Now she likes to host 'spiritual' events that honor our divinity.

Understanding the world beyond the ego and primal desires in herself and her clients has been fascinating. Learning and experiencing the richness of spiritual knowledge, practice, and diverse philosophies about life in deeper realms and higher states have been inspiring. After her illness, she was forced to simplify everything. To get grounded, she stopped all discovery and began purification. She has filtered out the delusionary and entertaining aspects of spirituality and found the essence of nature so beautiful. Helen teaches and shares this beauty wherever she can.

Journey of Discovering the Greatness Within

Born in Zimbabwe and groomed in South Africa by Greek Cypriot parents. Through her parents, she was exposed to the passion for life.

Being African was an education in itself with gender, race, and economic disparity; she became conscious of diversity and inclusion in childhood. She felt guilt for benefitting from her white skin and was determined to contribute to the world in whatever way she could. Life was very kind to her, with influential parents at her side. Her mom's name is Aphrodite, and her dad is Andrew. Both pioneering and entrepreneurial, she learned so much about drive and focus. Helen became a serious dreamer devoted to making a difference by discovering ways to work creatively with psychology. Drumming sounds and creative modalities built her a reputation in 14 countries as a pioneer.

175

It wasn't until her breast cancer diagnosis that she began to see the deeper purpose of her spiritual and emotional development training. She agreed to a mastectomy, one of the most significant moments of acknowledging the body's existential power and the feminine! Humbly, she realized life was not under our control.

Severing a body part is like editing a piece of history; a part of who you are dies, a program is deleted or archived.

After exposure to patriarchal structures, the gender divide perplexed her for 40 years, especially as an alpha female. She knew the lifelong search into her Ancestors, and her island of 10,000BC - that was patronized by the goddess her mother was named after (Aphrodites) - was all destined. Helen was a continuation of a legacy of priestesses from this island that played the drum in honor of the divine feminine principle. She was Aphrodites' daughter! That must mean something, right?

Paradoxically, we fulfill some soul contracts even if we don't know why. Events can happen paradoxically, like having a breast cut off. Her breast removal reminded her of the Amazonian warrior women in the ancient Greek myth. Who removed their breasts in defiance of male egos so they too could be brilliant archers for the war against injustice?

Suffering is a conduit for wisdom. When you command your life lessons to come through joy, that's when it will happen. Ten years after her divorce and many empath-type self-sacrificing relationships with men later, she realized she comes first. Men are not to blame but do need re-education from women. Healthy, strong women who can forgive and equanimously teach society the divine feminine and sacred masculine pathway to higher consciousness.

All the years devoted to revealing women's strengths on their life journey, she 'synergized' her common purpose with many global female leaders and built Women of Truth. A testimony to reconnect women to their spiritual legacy.

176

Spiritual meditating 'downloads' from a disturbing illness revealed the toxicity, injustice, and challenges of living on our planet. She galvanized a level of distributional leaders in all the world's experts to restore justice and cultivate emotional maturity and integrity on our planet. She met her soulmate life partner that she waited for her whole life. A man steeped deep in respect for feminine queendom now symbolizes the 'Amrit' nectar of a higher love. She knows women need to develop themselves first to activate their higher destiny.

Helen with her African Djembe drum from Ghana

Empowering Results

- Put over 160 women on stage as speakers, role models, and community leaders.
- Helped many families restore balance and harmony from chaos at home by supportive interventions or with their child with special needs.
- Developed a form of Drum Therapy as an innovative way to develop communities and assist conflict between Greek and Turkish Cypriot youth, increase

communion, address special needs, and integrate educational processes.

- Supported many individuals to discover and strengthen their inner freedom and wisdom.
- Run virtual and in-person gatherings on divine femininity and spiritual feminism resulting in deep conversations about self and others.
- Ran four conferences in Cyprus and Netherlands with over 200 participants to grow insights and personal realizations that make their lives more meaningful.
- Train and develop leaders, speakers, authors, and business owners to become strategic in their visibility.

Helen started a movement for female power and gave hope to women that there is the possibility of personal and professional development.

The Importance of Women's Contributions

Many women in antiquity had roles as leaders and custodians of the ceremonial, sacred altar-based activities, and activation thereof—divine intelligence and intelligence of what we regard divine pulsed through them. Transmitting and communing with the invisible realms of existence and the primordial 'rhythm of life itself, these women were the rhythm keepers of the rhythmic wisdom of life. Priestesses honoring the divine feminine principle of existence were in sync with the divine essence of the divine feminine. Nothing less than spirit-based leaders working on the unified field. Many women have this capacity through the power of intuition and their embodied wisdom. Life-changing wisdom born from life's challenges mix with bodily sensations that guide and advance a woman's path to need fulfillment and self-actualization. This is a type of emotional intelligence passed down from generation to generation (Redmond, 1997).

Women need reminders of this wisdom, and they need to have it shared with the world. "What the world needs now is feminine wisdom," to have their leadership bless the world. To nurture, guide, and support harmony and balance with planetary resources to create synergies that can help solve some of the world's other global changes. Public speaking leverages visibility and increases client attraction for those women that feel their wisdom could help wake up the world. Women elevate their unique intelligence to speak as paradigm shifters with authority and credibility to advance global change.

Integrating spiritual and psychological teachings on Divine Feminine Leadership led Helen to develop a formula for 'The New Femininity.'

Greatest Achievement

Nominated for Female Civility Award and Women Vision Award Awarded U.N.D.P.

Winner of the UNDP Small grant for Peace-building and Exceptional Women of Excellence Awards. All three of these life moments connected her to a world community of people that she felt mirrored her deepest heartfelt love for the world.

An Inclusive and Diverse World

What experts call diversive thinking is one of our most creative brain functions. Most of us are born with it. After some time in a formal educational setting, we lose the capacity to think up new ways to experiment with the world and its 'objects.' If we could get back our creative thinking ability, it would help us solve problems, quantum leap out of our comfort zones, and strengthen our flexibility. These are fast becoming a vital capacity for living in a changing world; neuro-agility.

1) An exercise you gain insight from is to put an object in the middle of a circle and ask each person to find a

unique purpose for the object. This will harness the power of diversity and inclusion for innovation. Here are more:

"Different roads sometimes lead to the same castle."

There are many ways up a mountain, and we often mislead ourselves and others glamourizing one way.

2) Ask every member of a group what they agree on to feel safe and see all the options. Look deeper and see that feeling safe is actually what we all agree on, but each one has a unique way to get there.

3) Gather in a circle; each person in the group is allowed to ask the group to participate in a reasonable moral fun action. The group results are positive instead of the normalized resistance, debate, or hesitancy. When all agree to respond with "Yes, lets," this is when the magic happens. This practice in improvisational theatre training teaches the power of collective agreement and consensus. It aids in the creative process while also giving each person the power of individuality.

"One of the greatest regrets in life is being what others would want you to be, rather than being yourself."

Tuning in to your own natural impulse to express something within you is much like how and why every blade of grass and every fingerprint differs, offering a distinct feature up to the global canvas of life.

4) Ask yourself, what would your future self-want you to do now, who are you becoming, and how do you get there from where you are now?

"It is time for parents to teach young people early on that in diversity, there is beauty, and there is strength."

5) Look into the uniqueness of each one of your group members and share from the heart something you would like them to honor in you. When we find distinctive details

that make us and others unique and share those, the whole universe opens up to us as a macrocosmic force that holds nothing but possibility.

Women of Truth Conference, Limassol Cyprus 2019

Strategies to Succeed in Our COVID Changed World

As the world changes, we must change with it. During these recent changes, Helen offered:

Online intuitive summits that included psychoeducation and therapeutic support, crisis management, change management, free enneagram neurosis, and personality training.

Hosted a platform for many women to collaborate, share their views, and guide others about keeping the faith and loving each other in critical times.

Perseverance and Determination is the spearhead of the arrow of intention that hits its target every time.

Author's quote

"We are the ones we have been waiting for, and what we are seeking is always seeking us!" Helen Argyrou

Bio

Helen Argyrou is an innovative Clinical Psychologist, Peak Performance Expert Strategist, and Speaker Change Leader. After becoming a drummer and building a creative drum therapy modality titled Druminspire, her fascination with rhythm affecting consciousness inspired her journey into neuroscience which resulted in her pivoting her expertise into Peak Performance. This fascination with the brain and peak states led her to develop a special talent in integrating science and spirituality. Helen expresses this by revitalizing education in various online summits, coaching pioneers and leaders in the lockdown-inspired Leadership Chamber and elevating new styles of thinking in her projects. The latest example is her WOMEN OF TRUTH movement that focuses on integrative health expertise by global leaders revolutionizing the future of women's health. After interviewing about 100 awakening female leaders and her signature message in an upcoming book, 'Why Down is the new up.' Please stand by for her women's wisdom book revealing the biggest lie women believe and the truth.

Learn more about this author

www.helenaha.com

Chapter 16

Changing the Paradigm in Global Population Health via Emerging Tech

Ingrid Vasiliu-Feltes, MD, EMBA
Healthcare Executive, Futurist, and Globalist

Introduction

Dr. Ingrid Vasiliu-Feltes is a healthcare, precision medicine and deep tech executive, a passionate educator, coach, mentor, entrepreneurship ecosystem builder, expert speaker, board advisor, consultant, futurist, and globalist dedicated to digital and ethics advocacy.

Ingrid has received several awards for excellence in research, teaching, and leadership throughout her career. This past year she has been named one of the Top 100 Women in Leadership Award, Top 100 Global Healthcare Leaders, Top 100 Global Finance Leaders, and Top 100 Women in Crypto.

Mission

Dr. Ingrid Vasiliu-Feltes mission is to redefine global population health via large-scale digital identity adoption powered by blockchain technologies and artificial intelligence.

All her current initiatives in the for-profit or not-for-profit arena revolve around emerging technologies, inclusion, and sustainability. Her mission is to impact society at a global scale by promoting education for science and technology, empowering young leaders to embrace innovation, collaborating with other key stakeholders globally to design novel technology-powered solutions for problems that have plagued our society for centuries. My mission has been to leverage and deploy the combined power of blockchain and AI to optimize global population health.

Vision

Dr. Ingrid's vision is to redefine global population health, putting the digital era's new products to full use. It is her vision, that only by leveraging emerging technologies across all domains within life sciences and healthcare, such as wellness, longevity, disease prevention, diagnosis, chronic disease management, and rehabilitation, as well as for research it will be possible to change the paradigm and outcomes for future generations.

"You do not know how far you can fly until you spread your wings and try" by Napoleon Bonaparte

Admiration of a Visionary Leader

Dr. Ingrid Vasiliu-Feltes identifies with Marie Curie, a Nobel Prize Winner. She admires Marie's innovative genius, courage, and determination to be a disruptor in an era where few women dare to dedicate themselves to science.

Journey of Discovering the Greatness Within

After 20 years of a dedicated career in life sciences and healthcare, Ingrid realized that she enjoys innovation and disruption. Her challenge was to balance her passion for sciences and academic pursuits with her relentless drive for digital transformation and interest in emerging technologies.

The tough spots throughout the years ranged from working 100-120 hours/week for many years, countless nights on call on service in the hospital, sacrificing time spent with her family, and constantly postponing career development opportunities.

The key lessons learned over the years were that our health is paramount, we can never regain quality time lost with our family, and that accepting mentorship or geocaching early in our career is crucial.

Empowering Results

Dr. Ingrid's approach to nurturing others has been to empower women via coaching, mentoring, and educational activities focused on financial acumen. She helps and educates women with negotiation, mediation skills, and stresses the need for digital literacy and fluency in today's highly technological landscape.

In Dr. Ingrid's experience, coaching women to identify their strengths is one of the best starting points. Once people know their strengths, she encourages them to develop a career to maintain their identity and integrity. She recommends adopting a moonshot thinking style as it is very beneficial. She also believes that disrupting the education systems is key to building a legacy of equity. She sees early education and mentoring as having a positively profound, long-lasting impact on women's careers.

The Importance of Women's Contributions

On a societal level, it would be helpful to focus our efforts on gender-agnostic early education and encourage a profound change in gender-biased parenting practices. From a business perspective, a focus on finance and negotiating skills would be essential for supporting many women that wish to attain the C-level in their career journey.

The main initiatives that Ingrid is involved in are the support for women revolving around education, coaching, mentoring, and financial inclusion. This support occurs through various roles she holds with international organizations. Some of these organizations include Women in AI, Inspired Minds, World Business Angels Investment Forum, and the recent Womenomics initiative by GCPIT (Global Cloud Platform Information Technology).

Ingrid is a volunteer and has been in leadership roles in over ten international not-for-profits that facilitate the achievement of SDG17 (Sustainable Development Goals 17). She is a critical influencer on several projects aiming to address the needs of startups, scale-ups, and SMEs (small and medium-sized enterprises). Ingrid has a global impact on education, entrepreneurship, digital advocacy, ethics, and women leadership.

Greatest Achievement

Ingrid, like most visionary leaders, has a long list of accolades. The diligence and forward-thinking in her research, teaching, leadership, and work experience reflect on her excellence. These awards and nominations are all well deserved.

> WBAF World Excellence Award-Social Entrepreneurship 2021
> Top 20 Global Leaders in Digital Twins Technologies
> Top 25 Global Leaders in Quantum Technologies
> Top 50 Global Leaders in Health Tech
> Top 50 Global Ecosystem Leaders

An Inclusive and Diverse World

Diversity and inclusion are key to improving decision-making capacity and generating more creative ideas. They are conducive to designing novel sustainable business models and have been shown to ensure a higher adoption rate for transformative products and services due to a more human-centric approach.

Women are key stakeholders in our quest to design and build a new Global Health Ecosystem. Women represent 70% of the global health workforce as per a recent WEF report titled "Delivered by women, led by men: a gender and equity analysis of the global health and social workforce." This report highlights women's important role and the challenges that need to be overcome related to leadership diversity and inclusion. This report called attention to the occupational segregation, gender pay gap, gender inequities that are systematic and require a novel approach. Gender-transformative policies need to be developed in collaboration with global stakeholders. They are essential to advancing gender equality in the health and social workforce. Another recent WEF report acutely points out the pandemic has prolonged the timeline to close the global gender gap [Global Gender Gap Report 2021]. Educating and training the next generation of healthcare workers to meet the skills demanded by the digital era is paramount for a thriving Global Population Health Ecosystem. Key stakeholders have a unique opportunity for visionary, inclusive, diverse, and ethical leadership to drive new novel educational initiatives and redesign training and development for a global workforce.

In her experience, the most helpful methods to foster diversity in innovation have been the deployment of design thinking methodology, embracing an abundance mindset, as well as fostering exponential and moonshot thinking.

Strategies to Succeed in Our COVID Changed World

During COVID-19 it was more important than ever to engage in global networking efforts, embrace transformation and disruption, apply design thinking methodologies, and encourage exponential thinking. Having the greater good for all society in mind and adopting an abundance mindset has been essential for reshaping and recalibrating the global economic recovery process. The future of education, work, travel, and how we conduct business has changed; they will never be the same.

The healthcare industry is plagued with challenges. Such as redundancy, inefficiency, waste, and high costs. Poor interoperability, sub-optimal data governance, and storage. There are ongoing adverse side effects due to errors, sub-optimal safety, long research and drug development cycles, poor access, lack of scalability for precision medicine solutions, and the ironic lack of a human-centric design.

Health Tech for Good

The industry is fraught with many challenges as well as opportunities. This 2020-2021 pandemic has exponentially accelerated the advent of the digital era. The world has a unique opportunity to redefine, redesign and reconfigure global wellness, longevity, population health, and delivery systems.

Some technologies that have not made it to large-scale adoption yet have the potential to transform, disrupt and optimize the global population health ecosystem.

Specifically, emerging technologies such as AI (Artificial Intelligence), AR, VR, XR, Blockchain, Nanotechnologies, Wearables, Brain-Computer Interfaces, 3D Printing, Bio-Implants, Robotics, Next Generation Computing (such as Quantum, Cloud, Edge, Neuromorphic and DNA Computing) are all intriguing tools in a healthcare's futuristic tech portfolio.

While none of these emerging technologies represents a panacea to all these problems, their combined impact could transform and lead to an optimized global ecosystem. They are considered major game-changers by impacting all domains of the healthcare ecosystem.

Technologies have some disadvantages, and large-scale deployment will require refinement and time. However, if implemented wisely with appropriate digital ethics and data governance mechanisms, they could provide an optimized global health and wellness ecosystem for future generations.

The pandemic profoundly affected many lives globally. Currently, the world is experiencing the consequences of a global economic and public health crisis. This may trigger a renaissance in the arts, humanities, or medicine with a long-lasting impact on our society.

Let's hope to learn from the vulnerabilities and weaknesses exposed, correct the mistakes made during this pandemic and facilitate us to be better prepared to prevent the next one and potentially redefine our approach to disease, health, and wellness. Future generations need not experience the same failures in pandemic prevention and management.

If the scientific and medical community shared their data on a global platform, there would be less redundancy, higher efficiencies, and shortened solution timeframes. The advanced tools used for COVID-19 could be applied long-term for solutions for other diseases.

Healthcare lags behind other industries in many aspects painfully highlighted during the pandemic. Thankfully these other industries quickly pivoted to use their existing modern infrastructure to provide critical supplies.

These futuristic technologies have increased our access to information and sped up the deployment of much-needed medical devices in our desperate quest to control the devastating humanitarian and financial effects of this pandemic. Healthcare Futurists would even venture to envision the existence of state-of-the-art Smart Health Cities where digital healthcare twins, digital finance twins, and digital legal twins would be part of our daily lives.

To be successful, we must strive for unprecedented global cooperation that will prevail over other political or economic interests for the sake of saving humanity. We must fiercely fight for a society that will be more mindful in deploying global resources. Strive to create open-source scientific databases, offering access in global exchange for precision medicine solutions, and would aim to maintain wellness, prevent disease, redefine healthcare, and use the full arsenal of digital technology to improve global population health.

To mitigate against the risks of maleficent use of these emerging technologies, we must also be accountable as a society and devote resources to develop robust data governance models, digital ethical frameworks, and state-of-the-art cybersecurity programs. So, what are these Healthcare Innovations and how are they helping the pandemic now? What can we learn from this pandemic and how can we demand reinvention of healthcare post-crisis so that future generations do not have to experience this type of trauma and helplessness?

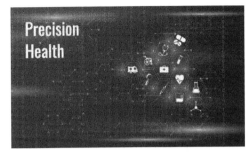

We have an opportunity to redefine wellness, redefine healthcare and improve global population health by designing state-of-the-art hospitals equipped with all the latest technologies available globally. We can truly disrupt old legacy "sick-care" models and focus on eradicating or preventing disease, delivering personalized care, never having to experience the embarrassment of not having protective equipment for our medical providers, and choosing which patient gets a ventilator or have no medications for our patients!

The non-healthcare giants have proven that their modern logistics and supply chain systems are much more effective, agile, and healthcare organizations need to seriously revise their strategic plans for the next decade (examples are Ali Baba, Amazon, Apple, Dyson, Google, Walmart, etc.).

As a society, we also have a moral duty to learn from this experience and demand a disruption of healthcare delivery models and healthcare supply chain systems and promote a shift from treating disease to preventing disease and focusing on wellness. This author believes that we have the unique opportunity to remove inter-disciplinary silos, share scientific advancements across geographic and institutional borders for all diseases, just like we have started to do during the current COVID-19 Pandemic.

One can envision a future global ecosystem built on a new exponential personalized medicine model that could offer future generations the human right of optimized population health. The journey is long; however, all the latest research points towards an accelerated adoption and a combined deployment of digital technologies towards building a highly performant Global Internet of Medicine, which could become the conduit for a Global Healthcare Ecosystem. By leveraging the full capabilities of these emerging technologies, we could achieve an exponential effect.

It is this author's sincere hope that after all the suffering experienced globally, we will experience a true rebirth of a global healthcare renaissance that future generations can cherish and benefit from.

Author's Quote

She often likes to share an insight with her colleagues and mentees. Perhaps she will be quoted someday: 'striving for excellence requires continuous sacrifices.' Dr. Ingrid Vasiliu-Feltes

Bio

Dr. Ingrid Vasiliu-Feltes, is a healthcare executive, futurist, and globalist who is highly dedicated to digital and ethics advocacy. She is a Forbes Business Council member, digital strategist, passionate educator, and entrepreneurship ecosystem builder. She is known as an expert speaker, board advisor, and consultant. She has received several awards for excellence in research, teaching, and leadership throughout her career. She is the recipient of numerous awards, most notably: WBAF World Excellence Award-Social Entrepreneurship 2021, Top 20 Global Leaders in Digital Twins Technologies, Top 50 Global Leaders in Health Tech, Top 50 Global Ecosystem Leaders, Top 100 Visionary In Education Award 2021, Top 100 Global Women in Leadership Award 2021, Top 100 World Women Vision Award, 2021-Innovation & Tech, Top 100 Women in Social Enterprise 2021 (nominee), Top 50 Global Thinkers (Nominee), Nations of Women Change Makers Award (finalist), Top 100 Healthcare Leader 2020 Award, Top 100 Finance Leader 2020 Award, and Top 100 Women in Crypto

2020. Additionally, she serves as an Expert Advisor to the EU Blockchain Observatory Forum and was appointed to the Board of UN Legal and Economic Empowerment Network.

Dr. Vasiliu-Feltes is CEO of Softhread Inc., the Founder, and CEO of The Science, Entrepreneurship, and Investments Institute, and currently serving as a Country Director for WBAF USA, Senator of WBAF, Faculty Member of the WBAF Business School- Division of Entrepreneurship and teaching the Executive MBA Business Technology Course at the UM Business School. She is also acting as the Chief Innovation Officer for Government Blockchain Association. Most recently, she served as President of Detect Genomix, Chief Quality and Safety Officer Chief and Innovation Officer for Mednax, Chief Quality and Safety Officer and Chief of Compliance for the University of Miami UHealth System.

During her academic tenure, she taught several courses within the Medical School, as well as the combined MD/PhD and MD/MPH programs. Throughout her career, Dr. Vasiliu-Feltes held several leadership positions and is a member of numerous prestigious professional organizations. She holds several certifications, such as Bioethics from Harvard, Artificial Intelligence and Business Strategy from MIT Sloan, Blockchain Technology and Business Innovation from MIT Sloan, Finance from Harvard Business School, Negotiation from Harvard Law School, Innovation and Entrepreneurship from Stanford Graduate School of Business, Certified Professional in Healthcare Risk Management, Fellow of the American College of Healthcare Executives, Patient Safety Officer by the International Board Federation of Safety Managers, Master Black Belt in Lean and Six Sigma Management, Professional in Healthcare Quality by the National Association of Healthcare Quality, Manager for Quality and Organizational Excellence, by the American Society for Quality, and Certified Risk Management Professional by the American Society for Healthcare Risk Management.

Additionally, Dr. Vasiliu-Feltes is an Honorary Advisory Board Member of several companies and an Editorial Board

Member for several international publications, an author, and a TV/Media partner.

She recently published a book with Dr. Thomason as a co-author on Applied Ethics in a Digital World https://www.igi-global.com/book/applied-ethics-digital-world/270860 and has three other books scheduled for publication in 2022 via IGI Global. :

Digital Identity in the New Era of Personalized Medicine

Impact of Digital Twins in Smart Cities Development

Impact of Women's Empowerment on SDGs in the Digital Era

https://linktr.ee/drvasiliufeltesmdmba

Dr. Ingrid Vasiliu-Feltes
Deep Tech & Precision Health
Exec. I Founder I Investor I Fo...

Chapter 17

Be Brave, Bold & Unstoppable: Live Your "Visionary" Dream Life

Rochel Marie Lawson
Founder of Bliss Full Living 4 U

Introduction

At 22, Rochel Marie Lawson became one of the first and youngest females to start a telecommunications installation company. She was moving into a male-dominated industry and could not get hired as an Electrical Engineer in Silicon Valley. Within four short years, she took that business from being unknown to one of the Top 50 Women-Owned Businesses in Silicon Valley. This business led her to become one of the few African American women who broke the glass ceiling that was once not an option for her, people of her race, or gender. The exciting fact is Rochel Marie envisioned herself being a successful business owner ten years before it happened. While playing a game with her girlfriends, she described the exact scenario of how she would become a successful entrepreneur and the age it would happen. This vision was just one of the many visionary experiences Rochel Marie shared with her girlfriends, and the best is yet to come.

Being a visionary woman leader does not happen when you become a woman. It begins to happen when you are a child. That little girl knows she has a purpose, and within that purpose, she can visualize what fulfilling her purpose and passion looks and feels like. As the little girl grows up, she discovers more about her sense, providing her with more future visions. Little girls that are leaders become women that lead. Women leaders with vision know that they are here to fulfill the image of their destiny within their purpose. Although they may not know what steps to take or what the road looks like ahead, they know that they are the only person in the universe that can turn their vision into a reality.

"I have always admired how Rochel Marie's vision for her life became a reality in her life. She is imaginative, intuitive, dedicated, determined, and an implementer. She takes action and helps others to do the same." Cecilia Jones

Mission

Rochel Marie Lawson, The Queen of Feeling Fabulous, is a Dream Lifestyle Transformation Facilitator. She works with women and men helping them unlock their bliss by balancing the pillars of wellness, wisdom, and wealth so that they can step in and live the life of their dreams. In her quest to support women worldwide, she has created The Brave, Bold & Unstoppable Women's Summit, held in venues around the United States. These events bring women together from all cycles in life, who are looking to support women on their quest to live a life fulfilling their passion, turning it into their purpose, and profit doing something they love to do. The mission of these events is to build a strong community of women around the United States and the world that are ready to support women in uplifting every aspect of their lives truly. The events empower, inspire, motivate, connect, support, and collaborate in a spirit of harmony that leads to strength, unity, and power that will change the world to make it a better place. Staying true to not leaving any woman behind, part of the proceeds from The Brave, Bold & Unstoppable Women's Summit supports our women veterans, our often-forgotten heroes.

Mission Statement: To create a solid and influential community of women worldwide that supports women in accomplishing their purpose.

She has already begun to create the Brave, Bold & Unstoppable community of women worldwide. Part of this mission is to be able to send a million girls around the world to college to leave no woman behind. This step will begin soon.

Vision

"I have often heard Rochel Marie say, "You cannot turn your dreams into reality without vision." Being a visionary leader requires taking action with your vision, and I know that without a doubt Rochel Marie Lawson is a visionary leader that's turned many of her visions into reality." She's a natural leader." Jules Walker

Vision Statement: To create a world where women are united in the spirit of harmony and balance, working together to create a world without discrimination, prejudices, violence, or death; A world where women support women and lift each other with inspiration, motivation, and action in a collaborative effort for the betterment of our society. A world where women live a life of their dreams filled with love, peace, wellness, wisdom, and wealth because that is the only thing to do.

Quote

"If you never try, you'll always wonder why. Take that brave step forward now and enjoy the powerful thrust of energy that it gives you, so you'll never have to wonder why." Ethel Bush

Admiration of a Visionary Leader

Rochel admires so much as a visionary leader who turned her vision into reality and helped many others do the same thing.

Harriet Tubman is the visionary woman that she admires. She was small in stature but was strong, determined, innovative, intelligent, intuitive, fierce, fearless, and unstoppable.

Harriet was a woman willing to take the risk to save her life and the lives of many others. She was a leader, a fighter, an organizer, a soldier, and a true survivor. She exhibited courage, and her willpower was unbreakable.

"Words of wisdom come from wise people that have lived the journey. I've known Rochel Marie since we were kids. Her love for Harriet Tubman has always been a part of her. When we were little, and things got tough, she always asked… What would Harriet do? This has been her motto for years and has led her to use her vision to become a reality in all that she does." Jacqui Johnson

When Rochel was a little girl in elementary school, Harriet was the first black person she remembered learning about, making Rochel very proud of her heritage. Before learning about Harriet Tubman, the slaves she had known about in school did not have names. They were just called slaves. Harriet was the first woman slave she learned about. This made her feel like she could do whatever she wanted as long as she stayed determined, persevered, and never gave up on accomplishing her dreams, even in danger.

Rochel's affinity, connection, and love for Harriet Tubman have grown stronger. She realized the monumental task Harriet accomplished with the Underground Railroad and how she continued to do amazing things as she trailblazed her way through life. Rochel has embraced and infused Harriet's spirit of determination, perseverance, courage, strength, innovation, focus, and never-give-up attitude into her life.

A woman faces challenges in a male-dominated industry that are similar to Harriet Tubman's difficulties with freeing slaves using the Underground Railroad. Rochel is the owner and founder of one of the first minority woman-owned telecommunications installation companies in the western region of the United States. She knows all too well what it takes for a woman business owner to be successful in a male-dominated industry.

There will always be obstacles and people who want to harm you and don't want you to succeed. However, she views these "challenges" as necessary evils that one must go through to fulfill their destiny and live the life of her dreams. Nothing worth having in life is easy, and just because a challenge appears on your path to "Bliss" does not mean that what you are doing or your vision in life is skewed. It means that you are in the right direction, and your destiny awaits you as long as you stay the course and continue your journey.

Now imagine having a very successful business, but when you checked in with your vision, you discovered that your image was that of a partial picture. It was not complete. Imagine realizing that the first business was just a part of the big picture of your visionary life. Imagine discovering that to continue the vision of your life, you had to start another business. It is a business that helps people step into living the life of their dreams, and this is your purpose.

This second business would be in a very traditional industry that would have to adjust to the new way of doing business. This business was going to be an online business, which meant changing the way business was done to the new way business was conducted.

Journey of Discovering the Greatness Within

To make your vision a reality, you will face some tough  decisions to continue your journey. With each opportunity to fulfill your purpose and destiny, there will be struggles that you have to overcome and difficulties that you will have to face. There may be things that you have to face about yourself that may not be pretty. To climb the mountain of success and be that leader who steps into greatness, you cannot skip over the not so "pretty" stuff about yourself. This information is a crucial ingredient for success.

Sometimes the biggest challenge you have to face begins with you. It starts with recognizing your weaknesses in addition to your strengths. Start with clearing out the "closet within your mind." Make space for the necessary items to assist you in being that visionary, cutting edge, and unstoppable leader you are or desire to be.

When Rochel started her first business, she was not in a perfect place with her physical health and well-being. She suffered from an undiagnosed digestive medical condition for about 14 years. The numerous doctors could not figure out what was going on with her or what caused so much upheaval, pain, and suffering in her physical body. This took a toll on her mental health.

Her physical health and well-being were unbalanced, and she became good at faking that she felt great. But she was so busy with her business, often submerged in her "work," she was distracted and numb from the physical pain that became a regular part of her day. Almost every day, she would wake up in pain.

The flip side was that she would cry herself to sleep almost every night because the pain she was suffering was so intense and unbearable. It felt like a raging fire burning her, trying to burn down the walls to get to the outside.

Every day she prayed for relief, prayed to be healed, prayed that the doctors would call and say... 'I know your trouble, and I know how to take away your pain.'

One day, everything changed. Her company was growing rapidly and was moving from a six-figure to a seven-figure business; she received a download during a meditation session. She had a vision of being pain-free, no longer suffering, and she needed to take the exact steps to make this a reality.

It took her back to her visionary leader Harriet Tubman because she would have visions about what to do when helping free slaves on the Underground Railroad. Her imagination led her to make the correct decisions to proceed forward. She never lost a slave and brought them all to safety and freedom.

After that meditation session, her life changed forever. During that time, the vision was the beginning of her becoming a visionary leader and inspired her to start her second business. Which is all about helping people live the life of their dreams by assisting them in the transformations necessary to make living a dream a reality. To do that, she focused on three pillars: wellness, wisdom, and wealth.

Empowering Results

Being a visionary leader who turns a vision into reality can be accomplished by anyone who desires to do so.

Here are a few tips that you can use to turn your vision into reality:

1. Believe, know, and own that you can achieve anything your heart desires.
2. Know that your vision is yours alone, and no one can make it a reality except for you.

3. Start with imagining yourself being that visionary leader you desire to be. Then add specific details to the vision by visualizing yourself doing what you're destined to do. This is important. Add as much detail as you can imagine. What are you wearing, the colors, what you're saying, who is present, time of day, weather conditions, location, how the place looks, an office, conference room, etc.? The more specific information you can add to the vision, the more natural it becomes and the more likely it will turn into reality.

4. Define the goal or goals that you want to accomplish. Write them down and view them often so that when times get challenging, re-reading your goals will fuel you with unstoppable energy.

5. Identify key members that you may need to add to your team to help you accomplish your goal of turning your vision into reality and assemble the team. You don't need to be the Lone Ranger and do it yourself.

6. Take Action. This is where most people fail. They neglect to take action because they become afraid and let the fear of failure stop them. Please note that there is no failure when you step into the role of turning your vision into reality. The only failure that happens is when you fail to take action.

7. Lastly, pay attention to the "markers" on your road to becoming that unstoppable visionary leader. Don't be afraid to pivot and course-correct if necessary to stay true to your path and yourself in becoming and being that innovative leader, you're destined to be.

Remember, visionary leaders come from all walks of life. It does not matter how much money you have or don't, how much clout you have or not, or how little you know about the road ahead of you. You need to understand that no one on earth can do what you are here to do or like you can do it.

If you genuinely desire to be a visionary leader that turns your vision into reality, then step out on that ledge and take that step of faith. Watch what unfolds in your life when you say "yes" to yourself!

Performing exceptional services for the world is something that all women and men should strive to do. Giving less than your best is unacceptable if we want to make the world a better place. Although providing and coming from your best self can be challenging at times, it is essential to keep in mind that the challenge is meant to make you better. Women are the most powerful species on the planet. Standing in the light of your greatness aligns you with the exceptional, unique energy that you have. This is the energy you're meant to share with the world, and it is this energy that provides that platform for you to share with the world how exceptional of a woman you are. Extraordinary women must connect and interact with other incredible women. Don't settle for less than the best because you deserve the best. Always stand in your beautiful light and allow the grace of the exceptional being to magnetize those you are meant to serve.

Greatest Achievement

Becoming a Top 50 Women-Owned Business in Silicon Valley

An Inclusive and Diverse World

To become part of the solution of diversity and inclusion for women, Rochel made it a point to join organizations that lacked women or looked like her. She believes allowing people of all backgrounds, ethnicities, and genders to have experiences with each other allows people to become familiar with what may be unfamiliar to them. This allows the unknown to become more knowledgeable, creating a

203

different experience and perception of the interaction. The comfort factor plays a huge role in allowing voices to be heard of those who may have a difference of opinion or background. Often this gives a different perspective and aids in coming up with a solution that benefits all. Networking, volunteering, being active in the business community, teaching, and collaborating are some methods she has used to be inclusive. This allows her to harness the power of diversity, inviting innovation into her life. Helping others thrive, gender diversity, fostering life experiences, sharing new perspectives, encouraging an inclusive community increases a sense of belonging for everyone.

Strategies to Succeed in Our COVID Changed World

As a visionary woman that also happens to be very intuitive, she was able to see the trends of what COVID-19 was doing in other parts of the world. As the owner of 2 very different businesses, one with personal customer contact and the other strictly an online business, she had already implemented several health and safety policies for both companies. The guidelines were developed in 2016 and updated in 2018. These guidelines outlined employee and customer safety in case of an outbreak of the flu or some other viral condition.

When COVID-19 hit in 2020, her companies were prepared. The telecommunications company that is a customer interface business adjusted based on its protocols, and their customers began sharing these policies. The combination of the two health and safety protocols allowed the business to continue but at a slower pace due to limited capacities in the various companies.

We created little COVID-19 wellness packs for each employee to have with them. Each employee must have a box of KN95 masks, disposable gloves, hand sanitizers, tool bags, and goggles in their vehicles, and they are required to carry a backup pack of gloves, a mask, and a single hand sanitizer in their pockets. All equipment used is wiped down with a sanitizing wipe before being placed back into the tool bag. Each employee gets a batch of sanitizing wipes each week or as needed.

If anyone is not feeling well, they must stay home until they feel better. Suppose they have a fever or any respiratory symptoms. In that case, they must stay home for ten days and have a negative COVID-19 test before returning to work.

The well-being of all employees is her number one concern. This policy is taken very seriously, and each employee is held to a strict standard.

COVID-19 is not going away, so we have to learn how to work, be cautious, and be safe in today's working environment.

Author's Quote

We all have the ability; the difference is how we use it. You have the capability to do amazing things that only you can do. You are FIERCE, FEARLESS, & UNSTOPPABLE!

"Having a vision is beautiful. Magnetizing, implementing, and living that vision is magical." Rochel Marie Lawson - The Queen of Feeling Fabulous

Bio

Rochel Marie Lawson is on a mission to unite women worldwide. Women who are brave, bold, and unstoppable, ready to unlock their bliss and turn their passion into purpose and profit. By connecting, collaborating, inspiring, motivating, empowering, and networking in a spirit of harmony to change the world and make it a better place for the future generation of females.

She is known as the Queen of Feeling Fabulous. Rochel Marie Lawson is a successful business owner, Registered Nurse, Ayurvedic Health Practitioner, Dream Lifestyle Transformation Facilitator, a multiple #1 Best Selling Author on Amazon, a 2-time International Best-Selling Author, and author of 4 other best-selling books, including "Intro To Holistic Health Ayurveda Style. She is a speaker, radio show hostess, and the president of Blissful Living 4 U, which was founded to bring wellness, wisdom, and wealth into the lives of individuals seeking a holistic path to living the life of their dreams.

Rochel Marie's energy, guidance, and enthusiasm have helped thousands of people improve their wellness, wisdom (aka mindset), and wealth by utilizing ancient, holistic principles that unlock the access for transformation to occur. She has been named one of the Top 50 Women-Owned Businesses in Silicon Valley and the creator of The Brave, Bold & Unstoppable Women's Summit.

Her weekly podcast, The Blissful Living Show, has been going strong for over ten years. She's been a guest writer for several blog publications and a featured core blogger for The Wellness Universe. She has been quoted in the Huffington Post and featured on Fox, CBS, NBC, and several other prominent media publication outlets.

Rochel Marie has spent over 25 years assisting people to achieve, elevate and sustain wellness and wealth through wisdom to enhance the power of their minds. Then transform their lives with abundance, clarity, energy, happiness, joy, peace, vitality, creativity, wisdom, prosperity, success, and wealth. For more information, check out: www.blissfulliving4u.com

Rochel Marie Lawson is also a majority shareholder of All Day Cable, Inc. She has two dogs, a Chihuahua named Diamond "little bit" and an Australian Shepard named Beamer "Boo-Boo." She has a shoe fetish and loves to travel. She spends her time between the San Francisco Bay Area and San Antonio, Texas.

Learn more about this author by visiting:

www.blissfulliving4u.com

www.unstoppable-womens-summit.com

Listen to her twice-monthly live talk show on National Public Radio called Real Talk. This is a talk show for women about issues women face in today's world. Go to: www.blissfulliving4u.com/realtalk to find out the show's schedule.

The Blissful Living Show Podcast: www.blissfulliving4u.com/podcast

GENERATIONAL IMPACT

Chapter 18

Generational Impact

Dr. Khalilah Johnson
CEO of Power After Trauma

Introduction

Dr. Khalilah Johnson is a Trauma and Resilience Expert and Certified Digital Marketing Professional known as the Overconfidence Coach. She helps purpose-driven women overcome false humility and perfectionism to develop invincible confidence, break generational barriers, and build businesses that positively impact future generations.

Mission: Breakthrough barriers, build better businesses, and become bridges of hope to future generations through educational resources, training, and coaching programs that empower others to discover the greatest version of themselves—*unpacking the past to impact future generations.*

Dr. Khalilah Johnson is an Executive Coach, Communication Architect, and Trauma & Resilience Expert with a history of multi-generational trauma of her own. After years of suffering severe trauma starting in adolescence, she struggled with deep depression, sleep deprivation, and detrimental memory loss, resulting in her being diagnosed as permanently disabled. She went from being locked inside of her own mind and limited in speech to today, being an award-winning, powerful Inspirational Keynote Speaker, International Best-selling Author.

Vision: To empower others to break the bondage of inherited generational thinking, overcome the dysfunctional norms and break through ceilings of cultural conditioning.

"We delight in the beauty of the butterfly, but rarely admit the changes it has gone through to achieve that beauty." — Dr. Maya Angelou.

Admiration of a Visionary Leader

One of the great visionary leaders who has inspired Khalilah's life's Dr. Maya Angelou. The late Dr. Maya Angelou had incredible resilience, brilliance, confidence, and dignified defiance! These are admirable qualities Khalilah most admires. A woman who had experienced more than her share of tragedy, from being violated at eight years old and then taking on the debilitating shame that her voice is what killed her attacker after he was murdered in retaliation for her assault. She spent five years being silent in fear of her voice. Dr. Maya Angelou was a teenage mother and high school dropout with a history of suffering defeat after defeat. It would have been a safe bet to count her out, but she not only defied impossible odds, but she also broke records and ceilings.

Today we know her as the distinguished Dr. Maya Angelou, an American poet, ivy league professor, civil rights activist, and one of the greatest trailblazing thought leaders of our time. She won several awards and received over 50 honorary degrees. I love her quotes because every word written offers wisdom and healing. Through her unapologetic transparency, she never hid her light or the darkness of her past. Her transferable courage allowed Khalilah to walk in her truth minus the shame she once carried. It will never escape her how parts of their stories are so similar. Khalilah, too, experienced childhood abuse that distorted her self-worth and then became a teenage mother. Like Dr. Maya, Khalilah's grandmother was a significant part of her upbringing and provided her with order and structure.

Journey of Discovering the Greatness Within

Years of suffering from trauma left Khalilah with feelings of low self-worth, debilitating depression that interrupted her ability to sleep, think and speak with clarity. Combined with being in an abusive relationship, seeking professional help, then being misdiagnosed and overly medicated, she was in a prison of her mind. She would eventually be declared permanently disabled before seeking a more qualified opinion. At this point in her life, her future looked bleak, and overwhelming hopelessness clouded her desire to live. Everything around her confirmed her life was over, but something inside started to call her up. After she attempted to end her pain, she began seeing glimpses of her future. Khalilah would have daydreams of speaking profoundly from a stage. Her current condition said one thing, but internally something was rising to reveal to her there's more! Based on the doctor's report and her symptoms of severe depression and decreased communication, she should have just accepted her fate, but through divine intervention, she couldn't let go of hope. Today, many who know her find it hard to believe that she once had to rebuild her capacity for basic memory recall, functioning, and speech. It's nothing short of miraculous as she went from not being able to complete sentences to today being an award-winning motivational speaker and teaching students from all over the world. It's why one of her favorite quotes from Dr. Maya Angelou is,

"I come in as one, and I stand as ten thousand; I shall not be moved."

Dr. Khalilah once believed she was just another woman who repeated a long family history of generational tragedy, but today realizes she is from a long line of overcomers who, despite tragedy, refused to relent. And today, she is one of many who will continue to overturn tragedy into a legacy of triumph.

Dr. Khalilah helps others; it is heartwarming and provides hope.

"I once felt like parts of me were being suffocated. That's when I discovered Dr. Khalilah Johnson. Since then, my life has never been the same. I was able to identify the lies I once believed. I discovered how cycles of generational torment can keep us in mental and emotional bondage. After enrolling in her mentorship group and personal coaching, she challenged me to change my negative self-view, discover my purpose, freely walk in my identity and embrace the fact I'm powerful."

S. F.

Visionary Leaders are organized, persistent, enthusiastic, innovative, and willing to take risks. They're eager to listen to others and remain focused. Many of our future leaders have a little sparkle of charisma that has yet to come to its full brilliance.

Empowering Results

At the end of last year, Khalilah mentored a dozen women through her 90-day mastermind. Many women were hesitant to jump into entrepreneurship, but they found the courage to commit to the process. Boundaries and fears are hard to deal with, but it is possible. The last year has been like no other as she walked women through the process of confronting their fears head-on. They all came out on top, from publishing books to starting successful businesses; now, they exude a confidence that you would never have guessed existed before.

The Importance of Women's Contributions

I believe it is important to understand that we have the power to heal, birth, and strengthen as women. We are the mothers, sisters, and daughters of the world. Gentle and persuasive, yet powerful! We can give even in our lack. It is imperative for us to know our authority and identity. When we stand together, show up in our confidence, and position ourselves in leadership, we can shift nations.

Her greatest passion is for youth and women. Khalilah's programs are centered around helping women discover their divine identity to come into their greatest power and confidence.

When we are healed, everything we touch grows. She now creates events, programs, and workshops that develop women in healing, business, and unapologetically living their truth.

Greatest Achievement

One of her greatest achievements is when she randomly reached out to a young woman who weighed heavy on her heart and showed up at her house moments before she would have taken her own life.

She shared the details at a youth workshop, and Khalilah found herself mulling it over for months. What if she had ignored that inner prompting?

- A 90-year-old woman shared that she had never said aloud that she was hurt as a child until that conversation with Khalilah after she spoke at a church presentation.
- At a women's conference, she spoke for domestic violence awareness; a 75-year-old woman confessed to Khalilah that she was in an abusive relationship and was ready to get help.

Countless stories like this deepen her passion for walking in her purpose.

An Inclusive and Diverse World

Worldview: Being a visionary means seeing beyond sight. When developing solution-based products and services, include insight from people of different cultures and experiences. This not only encourages inclusion but increases wisdom by listening to other perspectives.

Unity: Challenge individual biases and find what unites us. The best way to create without exclusion or prejudice is to start with what brings us together - love for ourselves, family, friends, and community. We don't all have to believe the same things, but we can always find shared values.

Selflessness: Letting go of your feelings and putting yourself into someone else's shoes opens you up to a broader range of creativity and opportunity. Creating for others helps us understand their perspective on complex matters, and that understanding is crucial for real progress.

Connection: Innovation can become rigid and mechanical without connection. We're living in a time where artificial intelligence is soaring. We must be intentional about being generational bridges and building trusting partnerships.

Curiosity: Being genuinely interested in others can positively stimulate innovation, inclusion, and bringing people together.

What positive impact have you made in your community?

Dr. Khalilah has been nominated for Youth Leadership by the WWCA. She has served as a youth leader for several years, developed programs for emotional intelligence and suicide prevention, also serves as a trauma advocate who has supported others in receiving mental health and wellness service. She actively looks for ways to serve at-risk youth. She recently served as a recurring virtual workshop facilitator for the Maryland Youth Law and young teenage mothers transitioning from foster care. With honor, I will continue to serve my community.

Ways you motivate and encourage other women to achieve success?

Khalilah encourages women and survivors of abuse who are still not positive about trusting themselves to find ways they are encouraged, despite painful experiences or acknowledge things within them that make them feel victimized. When people cannot recognize the motives that drive them to perfectionism, they may be motivated to overwork themselves, or people please yet still never feel like they are doing enough. This often leads to a life of outer achievements but inner turmoil.

The only way to truly experience happiness is to do everything from the power of identity and purpose. When they stand on the foundation of worthiness, they stop seeking acceptance and are able to make an impact authentically.

Strategies to Succeed in Our COVID Changed World

Learning was always an important part of her life. Still, during the pandemic, she made it a priority to increase her skills in digital marketing and trauma support to help others adjust and survive while living and doing business in this new age. We need to be acquiring new skills that are necessary for growth; this shows determination. We must learn how to be resilient and persevere despite difficulties and find the advantages in the disadvantages.

Dr. Khalilah is now certified in multiple areas of Digital Marketing, Trauma Support, and Holistic healing with expertise in Google Ads, Copywriting, and Content Marketing to best serve clients. The recent devastation was a wake-up call for us, showing how quickly life can change forever.

Artificial intelligence software was already being developed, and the next decade was set to change how we do business. Fortunately, many servant leaders have re-calibrated our learning and awareness in time for the changes.

BIO

Dr. Khalilah Johnson is the CEO of Power After Trauma, Courage and Confidence Coach, Communication Architect, and Trauma & Resilience Expert with a history of multi-generational trauma.

In pursuit of a breakthrough for herself and others, Dr. Johnson is now a distinguished member of the American Academy of Experts in Traumatic Stress, collaborating with the National Center for Crisis Management. She is a Licensed Interfaith Chaplain and Doctor of Philosophy. She has over 40 specialists' certifications in the areas of holistic healing, psychology, trauma, marketing, and business.

Dr. Johnson teaches the same methodology she used to break free from a life sentence of a disabling, mental, and emotional prison through her signature program, UNPACK 2 IMPACT: The 5 E's of Effective Generational Transformation. In her programs, she has taught students from over 97 countries how to clear blockages of limiting beliefs, identify, and break intergenerational trauma patterns, turn purpose into profit and go from invisible to influential.

Her story has inspired millions globally and has been shared on Fox, NBC, CBS News, Chicago Tribune, Authority Magazine, and Thrive Global.

Chapter 19

The Old Way Is the Right Way

Barb Swan-Wilson
World-Class and Editor of Heart

Introduction

When you've been loved, cared for, and supported from birth to the present, it makes perfect sense to this author to acknowledge these blessings and respond in a similar fashion. Barb has worked in several diversified lines of work which gives her a unique knowledge base. She is open to hearing your story and point of view then assist you in getting your message delivered into the world. Barb gets your story to flow with words that will connect your message to your audience. Barb is excited about what the future holds for those stepping up and into their truth.

Mission

Barb has always had a caring heart and goes out of her way to help others. Over the last few years, she has helped hundreds of businesspeople get their stories out into the world. These stories and advice increase a businessperson's credibility. Many of the stories truly impact people to make changes and improve their well-being. Barb has been an editor with 1 Habit Press and recently joined forces with B-Global Publishing to assist authors in getting their message out into the world. Their focus is to lead by helping our world heal and for humankind to grow in understanding each other to live in harmony.

Mission Statement: To encourage and assist people in sharing their life stories of lessons learned to benefit others.

Vision Statement: To see the world come together to understand and accept our differences. With everyone working together through education, shared knowledge, and a common goal of peace.

Quote

"I am very cautious of people whose actions don't match their words." by Alex Elle

This quote may not sound very inspirational, but it is excellent advice to protect you. However, it is inspiring to find people whose actions match their words in integrity and overall intent of goodwill towards others.

Admiration of A Visionary Leader

 What greater visionary leader is there to have in your life other than your mother? Maureen (Swan) Kaiser is supportive in all Barbara's endeavors. When she thinks about her mother, she remembers her friends saying, "I wish your mom was my mom," and when someone wants a guide or a leader, and they share a sentiment like that, you have a true leader. Her words of "Sure you can" ring in Barbara's ears.

Maureen was involved in the community on many levels, always ready to lend a helping hand with a beaming smile. She was well-spoken, had a way with words, and had beautiful handwriting when she sent thank you letters. She was always welcoming and open to meeting new people and would be especially pleased if she had the opportunity to entertain them.

Barbara's mom was particular about routines and best methods, such as cleaning day every Saturday. Cleaning from top to bottom was the only way, and one should never mop the floor before dusting.

Maureen is an understanding person, a great listener, sounding board, empathic, willing to give people another chance, and firm on her beliefs.

Although Barbara was unwilling to adopt all her mother's attributes, she appreciates them all, especially her loving demeanor. Over the years, Barbara sees how her mother's influence has shaped her life and how she has adopted many characteristics (including her looks).

Barbara sees herself as someone who stands firm on her beliefs when she understands the situation and the facts. She sees herself as a good listener and welcomes new people in her life. She misses the open world where she could invite numerous people into her home and entertain them. Barbara is very stuck on functional and methodical things. Clean top to bottom - set systems in place and knows routines and good habits are critical to personal satisfaction and success.

Journey of Discovering the Greatness Within

Life provides opportunities and challenges, and sometimes they are one in the same. Barbara believes that each of us faces difficulty no matter who we are. She grew up with two parents in a nice home until her 14th birthday. The next day her dad left her mom. This was a shocking blow as she never heard her parents' fight. Emotions ran high, and in mom's frustration, she kicked out the glass patio door cutting her foot. Mom then locked herself in the bathroom. Barb and her younger brother felt their first moments of fear. Fear that mom would take her life. The worry and shaking they felt were new to them. How quickly life can change.

The next several years had lots of scary moments. Barb remembers her mom falling asleep while driving. She wasn't sleeping well and who would under the stress of divorce and figuring out how she would keep a roof over her kids' heads. Dad was helping financially, but the pressure was still there. What Barb learned was that she wanted to find a loving husband that would never cheat on her in the future.

Eventually, she found a man she believed would be faithful, and they married. There in came a new problem. Barb grew up without yelling and fighting and did not have the experience to deal with the barrage of almost daily yelling and then receiving the silent treatment. Emotional support was lacking. In hindsight, she should have left the marriage in the first year, but she did not want to be a divorcée.

Barb's dream was to create a decorating center to make people happy with color. She created Strokes of Genius. Her husband was not happy with her choice, and she remembers him saying, "If I knew you were going to open a store, I would never have married you." He did over the years help her with graphic design and newsletters, although she cannot remember him ever lifting a can of paint until the sad day came when she closed the store.

Running this store became her sanctuary, a way to stay away from him. She often worked late, and in the end, she got very sick, hospitalized, and came close to death. The first day she was in the hospital, she clearly remembers sending him and other family members away so she could be in peace. At that moment, there was a shift and acknowledgment that she needed to care for herself and not be supportive and positive towards others. She needed to survive. That night she almost died.

After nine days in the hospital, she came home with the surgeon's words ruminating in her ears. 'Close,' he said. What the heck did that mean? Later it was clarified, 'close' you didn't die or 'close' you didn't lose your leg. The surgeon says this, and the husband denies she almost died. Not a supportive environment.

Barb was weak and couldn't walk more than a few steps when she got home. It was her mom that often came to help her during the day. Over the next two months, Barb returned to her store but was full of anxiety and often cried for no apparent reason.

She found a Christian counseling service that helped her keep her life together. Through this counseling, she sorted out many issues and became strong. She even got off all the pills the doctors put her on and eventually left her husband and started a new life. Without getting sick and counseling, Barb thinks she likely would never have gained the mental strength to leave the marriage.

Barb has had support throughout her entire life, and it comes from her mother. There have been times that Barb did not want to speak with her mom, but she always loved her. In the mid-80s, when Barb was in university, she promised her mom that she would be there to care for her, and today she is. Barb had a plan to find work online to be flexible and work almost anywhere.

Caring for our parents in their elderly years seems to be a thing of the past. For whatever reason, many people put their parents in various types of homes where they may or may not get the best care. Barb believes that adult children should care for their aging parents in their homes for as long as possible. Make the end of their life as enjoyable as possible, and if they pass away at home with family by their side, that would be best.

Recently her stepfather passed in his home. Barb cared for him in his last few days and made sure to encourage her stepsiblings to come to see him when the end was near. He passed with his wife at his side, and a couple of his children arrived moments before he took his last breath.

The old way is the right way. Caring for those who cared and supported you just feels right. It is what has been done throughout most of history. However, it does not seem to be so in North America. Now Barb knows there are situations where there is not a choice, but it always warms her heart when the family does the right thing and cares for their parents.

It is five weeks since her stepfather passed away, and her mom is still mourning his loss. The stepchildren and Mom's eldest son show up at her home and tell her she has to be out of her home in 45 days. Mom is devastated and doesn't understand how this could be happening.

The very children she welcomed into her home 45 years ago, and her oldest son now want to evict her from her home of 60 years and put her in a supportive living home. Removing an 86-year-old widow from familiar surroundings is not a loving thing to do when two children are willing and capable to care for her. This is a heartless act and the wrong thing to do!

There have been two unnecessary and disturbing meetings at her mother's home in the past week—one for eviction, the other to send her mother to a home. The second meeting also included a death threat towards Barb. No one needs this added stress, especially to someone as vulnerable as a recent widow.

Barb's strength has been building since counseling. She has the strength to stand her ground against lies, bullying, and the life threat.

Barb hopes that her strong stance against such evil will lead others to stand up for what is right. When people stand in their integrity and stand up against the bullying, they can end the hate. Let your love shine light into the darkest crevices

Empowering Results

Genuine caring will lead to positive results. Barbara has helped many people in different ways, giving street people warm clothing and buying them meals. She created special and fun events for a group of people that are shunned by society. One of these people years later still says good morning and goodnight to her on Facebook messenger, and Barb replies.

Barbara has a can-do attitude and shares that attitude with others. It is our attitude towards most anything that influences the outcome. It can all look so much better when you shift your perspective and attitude.

When Barbara hires someone, their attitude greatly influences her decision. She once was approached by someone on welfare who requested to learn how to paint specialty faux finishes. This person wanted to get off social assistance, and their attitude won her attention. She admits she did test their resolve as she had a misguided preconceived bias against them but was willing to give them a chance. This young man became her decorating center's assistant manager within two years. He later moved on to be a talented graphic designer.

Barb created this decorating center to become the most helpful store for miles around. And people did come from miles around, and she was astonished at the distance some would travel. She was proud of her customer service level. She was honored when the co-author of the book Raving Fans visited her store. He later sent a signed copy of his book with a notation that he was a raving fan of her service.

This store had thousands of repeat customers. Why did they return year after year? Barb believes it was because she provided a solution to their problem. She took the time to understand the problem they faced, explained how to fix it, and showed them tips and tricks to make their project flow easier.

The store's personalized service provided a sincere environment of caring. On occasion, Barb went to a customer's home to view a challenge they had. It was a great place for advice, guidance, and top-notch products. Her mother was her greatest cheerleader and showed up to help almost daily. Customers could visually see that they were mother and daughter. Along the way, her friendly, outgoing younger brother joined the company. Customers appreciated the family atmosphere.

The glory of this busy shop came to a rather abrupt halt when the lack of self-care resulted in a nasty life-threatening diagnosis and a two-month absence from the business. Upon her return, her heart was no longer focused on helping others. She was focused on surviving as she now dealt with anxiety, panic attacks, and depression. Apparently, some of her customers were devastated at the loss of their favorite store. Barb was told customers cried at the door when they discovered the store was closed.

The Importance of Women's Contributions

The world is full of the good, the bad, and the ugly. Women can be part of all of these, but we are brimming with the good at our core. Women saved Barbara's life. Lying in a hospital bed, feeling her life slipping away, it was four angels - female nurses who were there rescuing her.

Women are inherently caregivers and bring a different perspective of the world. Often their viewpoint comes from a place of genuine caring and desire for solutions to the betterment of all involved. Our world is benefiting for the most part, where women are the leaders.

When women are educated and worldly-wise, their understanding and influence have dramatically positive effects. As the world and a great many leaders accept the powerful and positive influences women have, it is hopeful that more women and children will receive an education allowing the female voice to rise up and heal this world.

A piece of advice to the female gender of all ages is to stop watching the 'catty' reality TV shows. Find a mentor or coach who believes in you and has your best interests at heart. Get out into the real world and help others, even make a promise to a young girl, and join the Big Brother Big Sister Association.

Women make a difference in everyone's life. Without them and their natural instinct to protect our young, Barb is unsure where this world would be today. Small things can have an enormous impact, such as saying good job or a simple thank you to a woman or anyone. As you don't know what their life is like. Be kind, supportive, and follow through on your promises. Support women with positive statements on social media, avoid backstabbing, and gossip as it brings you down a few notches in your well-being, in the eyes of others, and is not helpful to anyone.

Greatest Achievement

Barbara's single greatest achievement was learning to step out of her comfort zone. She says it is scary every time, but life is an adventure, and she is an explorer. She learned to say yes; I can do that. She found ways to build businesses that many said could not be done. With $750 of borrowed money, she created a decorating center that her clients dearly loved. Years later, with no previous knowledge of the bowling industry, she rejuvenated a small-town bowling center into the fun spot it once was.

With the ability to step beyond her comfort zone Barbara has been the editor on the world's largest book on entrepreneurship and the fastest book ever published from concept to delivery in less than 18 days. Step out to step up.

An Inclusive and Diverse World

Barbara grew up in a world of white people. She knew one family of Asian descent, and at elementary school, there was one beautiful, smart black girl. A person might think she would grow up to be racist in such a one-sided world. But this was not the case. You see, while growing up, she had some learning challenges and was bullied. The kids who didn't pick on her became her schoolyard friends, and some also had challenges. These children were far more accepting of the differences amongst everyone. These kids were true friends, and they acted like friends. They were not just friends to your face then talk nasty behind your back. These experiences drew Barb to conclude that she needed to be somewhat wary of people and their words at a young age. "I am very cautious of people whose actions don't match their words" by Alex Elle.

Respect and acceptance of everyone were taught at home. With a caring, loving attitude, she ventured off into the world to discover this attitude was not one that everyone held. The gossip and backstabbing seemed cruel and unusual. She attempted to steer clear of people with these negative comments.

As she worked retail jobs, she saw how often people with a certain look would be shunned, receive poor service, or called names to their faces and behind their backs. She didn't understand how people could be so mean. Barb then started going out of her way to provide exceptional service to those she thought might not typically receive good service. Later in life, she would hire disadvantaged people to give them a hand up. Please note that disadvantaged people do not mean disabled; it means only someone who needs a little help because of some life situation or may not be as lucky as most of us.

Barb stepped out of her comfort zone to do something wonderful for her small-town community; she kept in mind how wonderful it would be to have the doors wide open to accept those less fortunate. The bowling center was open to everyone from 1-year-olds to 90-year-olds, and everyone had a blast. The hours were long, and the income was short. But her very favorite night of the week was when the clients of the Abilities Center came down to play. They had fun together, and there were no hidden agendas. We were a bunch of happy people doing what happy people do - smile and laugh. Barb will cherish those special evenings and is thankful she could give them the special attention they deserve.

1. Don't pre-judge people, and if you do, back up and start again. You don't know what someone's life is like or the challenges they face.
2. Treat everyone with kindness and respect.
3. Listen to understand and show your caring heart; we all have our troubles and, at times, need someone to listen.
4. If money is your driving force, treat everyone like they are worth a million bucks. If money is not your driving force, good for you but still treat everyone like they are worth a million bucks!
5. Be open to possibilities as the perspective view of someone else may create a chain reaction of new ideas and solutions that were not known before.

Strategies to Succeed in Our COVID Changed World

When you believe - you can achieve! Barbara has been vetting various online products and services for almost a decade. Over these years, she has found some life-changing products and, of course, some duds as well.

Barbara has a philosophy that if she is going to promote anything, she has to try it and approve it for herself first. She has amassed a group of products that are proven winners and shares them with others when she can provide a solution for someone, whether for a business or personal.

At the beginning of the 'plandemic', she was in physiotherapy recovering from a shoulder injury. Like most of the world, she was struck with fear, and access to her gym was denied. Unable to do anything that required physical strength, she turned to the internet to learn. During an online business summit, she met someone unlike anyone else she had ever met. This person was so real and was changing Barbara's perspective on life within minutes.

As downtrodden as Barbara felt, she reached out to this magical person who ignited a spark within her. When a person is feeling down, it is advantageous to volunteer to help others, which she did. Barbara offered to help the celebrity, Forbes Riley. This has become a story in itself for another time, but for now, it has changed Barbara's life and career focus.

When you are isolated and feeling down without much hope (but there is always hope), the way up is the way out. That's right, get out of your comfort zone. Go and learn something new. Barbara's strategy during the COVID years was to learn as much as she could about working and helping others to succeed online. She is a thought-driven entrepreneur who will soon release a Metaverse business.

Author's Quote

"I can do, and I am doing." Barbara Swan-Wilson

She says these words several times a day as it keeps her open to her unlimited potential, along with her mom's words ringing in her ears, "sure you can."

Bio

Barbara Swan-Wilson is known as the editor with heart. Barb gets your story to flow with words that connect your message to your audience. She is open to hearing your story and point of view then assists you in getting your message delivered into the world. She is excited about what the future holds for those stepping up and into their truth.

By rediscovering her purpose and rekindling the entrepreneurial fire, she is now on a mission to help you, the business owner. She writes and or edits weekly emails for her clients. She can publish your stories, build your creditability, brand your company, and help you build your dream.

Barbara is an honors graduate of Commerce, Industry, Sales, and Marketing and has always had a keen interest in marketing and advertising. As a life-long learner, she has completed dozens of courses from Project and Risk Management to Forbes Riley's OPP. She has operated two well-received companies and has thousands of happy "Raving Fans." She was awarded the self-employment 'Excellence in Entrepreneurship in 2000.'

Connect with author:

https://www.facebook.com/barb.swanwilson

https://www.linkedin.com/in/barb-swan-wilson-9812022b/

Chapter 20

Mission to Millions

María Angélica Benavides, EdD
Ultimate Legacy Builder, A World-Class Storyteller,
Serial Entrepreneur, and Publisher

Introduction

Dr. Maria Angelica Benavides is known as the Ultimate Legacy Builder, and Dr. B. who is well-known as a global publisher, a visionary woman leader, networker, speaker, and educator. She is a mover, a shaker, and a change maker. She is passionate about serving all students, including students with special needs, through an online academy and entrepreneurship career path. Her bigger goal is to live and leave a legacy for generations to come. THROUGH EDUCATION AND CONNECTIONS, Dr. B. supercharges women business owners' mindsets and finances. She adds a beautiful component of spiritual service, helping all individuals align with their higher self through metaphysical practices and tools.

You would be surprised how your inner fear can trick you into believing beliefs and limitations that you can overcome. Fear can make you believe you can't master what you think you hate. When in fact, what you once hated can turn into a passion and business. Angelica said, "Boy, I hated writing and school. I was born in Mexico, with Spanish being my first language." Now education is a major focus of her life.

As a little girl, she was very shy and introverted; now, she is outgoing and loves much of what she once hated. Angelica had a big imagination, which led her to become a global publishing company.

Mission

Dr. B helps women spread their message through storytelling and delivering the right message to the right audience. She inspires and motivates women entrepreneurs to write books that outlive them. And help them align to their best version of who they are and who they need to become to achieve the bigger version of themselves. Dr. B's is supercharging women business owners to take big ideas into reality and help them step into their greatness.

Mission Statement: Dr. B. helps women clarify and establish a mission for millions to be delivered to millions of people around the world to raise awareness, empower people into leadership, and elevate them to serving millions.

Vision

A visionary women leader must take responsibility to create a mission and legacies that will take our future generations to places we never imagined we could reach.

Core Values

1. Purpose
2. Hope
3. Inspiration
4. General Impact
5. Lasting Connection

THROUGH STORYTELLING, Dr. B. is the founder of B-Global Publishing to supercharge women business owners, delivering the right message to generations to come. Elevate your business by using the power of storytelling and connect it to your mission to connect and establish authority! The right mission and story are an opportunity for those who are dedicated to changing the world.

Dr. B. shows women entrepreneurs how to scale their businesses, educate them to become financially literate and use financial knowledge to make better decisions from everyday spending to long-term financial planning. Throughout the chapter in bold words Dr. B. will share her key recipes to help you share your Mission with Millions.

"The only thing worse than being blind is having sight but no vision."   *Helen Keller*

Admiration of a Visionary Leader

Dr. B admires many visionary women leaders. One that she admires is Forbes Riley. Angelica met her about a year ago when she signed up for the Forbes Pitch Masterclass. She immediately loved the boldness, bravery, and strong connections she created with her clients. She is a dynamic woman who is very compassionate and truly cares for those that cross her path. She has sold more than $2.5 Billion of products, and now she teaches her secrets on how to pitch most anything. bestselling books and the most amazing training classes.

Forbes is not an ordinary person, which makes Dr. B think bigger and take big action steps first key to spreading your Mission to Millions. To give you an example of how fearless she is, Forbes had a unique way of remodeling her house. The movie Die Hard exploded her house in Los Angeles. Forbes goes beyond "normalcy." She amazes Dr. B all the time as she gets to know her more. Dr. Angelica Benavides admires her boldness and going the extra mile and wants to model herself after. She serves millions, and for Dr. B to serve millions, she will follow what Forbes says as she has left successful tracks for millions of people to follow. Connect with Forbes and read her chapter to follow her. Dr. B feels blessed to have met Forbes and be part of her community. Forbes wrote a chapter for this book because she believes in her students. She is Angelica's role model.

The other amazing woman Dr. B. honors and loves dearly Sofia her mother. Without her mother Dr. B. would not be here. Her mother was a very simple woman who had 11 children. Sofia had no education but had an inner wisdom that guided her to raise her 11 children. Her mom was very focused on raising her children and was a stay home mom. She still did menial jobs like washing clothes for other women. She was very creative and worked on arts and craft. D. B got the side hustle syndrome from her. She did what it took to raise her kids and make money. Her mom didn't know English well, but it didn't stop her. She went to school to learn how to speak English. She didn't master it, but it is finding the tools to help you navigate life that counts. Navigating life and finding the tools and resources you need is another key on how to get your mission to millions.

Journey of Discovering the Greatness Within

Dr. Angelica Benavides's (Underwood) business was born from times of uncertainty. She is living a life that defies the odds. She was the ninth of eleven children born to Mexican immigrants. She struggled in the English (monolingual) classroom and often doubted her ability to succeed. As a native Spanish speaker, Angelica struggled in all her classes - especially reading. Angelica was the first in her family to finish high school, but even on her graduation, she wondered. "How did that happen?" After finishing high school, Angelica took menial jobs that did not require much education. She felt that, despite her diploma, she probably would not amount to much. Fortunately, one of her employers saw in her what she did not see in herself: potential. Armed with confidence, she enrolled in Laredo Community College and earned a doctoral degree in Leadership and Specialized in Curriculum. Dr. Angelica has proven that success is possible for everyone by creating a plan and sticking to it through thick and thin!

Dr. Angelica has gained the unique ability to help people release the mental obstacles that prevent them from achieving their very best at work, in business, and life. She is committed to empowering others to exchange the chaos of life for the best life possible. Helping people unlock their full potential and believing their time is now. She shares her personal story on how she beat cancer and how to heal your body and your life. She shares some of her challenges in life and how she overcame the darkest moments of her life, turning them into light, joy, love, and empowerment. Dr. Angelica is committed to providing a RoadMap to her online coaching platform. You connect with other passionate women and unique voices who share their challenges and how they overcame life challenges. Dr. Angelica empowers women in all areas of life, such as health, money, relationships, education, and career, by teaching you universal laws and how to play the game of life. Life is simply a game you must learn how to play to achieve your highest potential and live on purpose to be self-actualized.

Dr. Angelica Benavides (Underwood) lives a life that defies the odds. She has become an influential and global leader helping women regain their power, voice, choice and take action toward their dreams to thrive.

After healing from two types of cancer, losing two homes, bankruptcy, divorce, and her world tumbling down around her, she discovered she has a bigger purpose in life. She now shares her impactful story and influences women worldwide to never give up. Now she is committed to a mission to serve millions of people worldwide, encouraging them to live and leave a legacy that outlives them.

Empowering Results

Dr. B. has been touching lives for more than 30 years as an educator. Accomplished, strong, and dynamic educational leader with high ethical standards. Dr. B can help small business owners and school districts create and implement systems, policies, and procedures. She aims to provide direction on developing extraordinary site-based programs supporting all students and entrepreneurs around the world. She has a book series, From Zero to Success where authors from all over the world share their mission to millions on how they started from scratch to where they are now. Experienced in working in a richly diverse school community with bilingual skills; she successfully leads major organizational change; strong

community partnership; demonstrated experience in collaboratively working closely with leaders and supporting initiatives and priorities aligned with implementing a rigorous curriculum to prepare students for success. Dr. B has the ability to prepare and deploy a Strategic Plan and create a mission to serve millions by working collaboratively with multiple and diverse constituencies and departments. If you have no vision and plan, you have no clear direction. You will end up going in circles or feel stuck. A Strategic Plan is key, so you have a sense of direction and outline your measurable goals. Strategic planning will help guide your day-today decisions. You can evaluate progress to change your approach if it is not working or if your plan works duplicate and use it repeatedly because you have found a Formula that Works!

Greatest Achievement

One of her greatest achievements in her lifetime is living! She was able to outlive two types of cancer. Before being diagnosed with cancer, she was doing Zumba, and six inches of her intestines twisted, and she nearly died at that time. During one of her surgeries in dealing with cancer, she ended up with a blood clot that led to a severe infection landing her in intensive care for more than a week. Her greatest achievement and honor are being alive. She realized she had a bigger mission, to share with women leaders around the world to live their life's purpose in a bigger way. Dr. B. discovered in her life journey that to achieve big dreams. You must take big risks. It is scary but Bravery is key. You must simply do it and take actions towards your big dreams to achieve any success. Getting a message in front of millions might not be easy but it is possible.

Create a mission for millions. Make sure to write a book that outlives you. Live and leave your message and story that are your golden nuggets on how you overcame challenges in life. So, our children, children, and future generations are inspired to keep going no matter how difficult life might seem. We need to encourage and inspire people to find love and joy within. We must celebrate small wins to motivate us and create momentum in our life. Remember to be present in all your life experiences. It is not the destination you seek but the experience of the journey that is brought to your soul. Collaborate and build strong relationships to have a sense of belonging and create supportive communities.

An Inclusive and Diverse World

An inclusive and diverse world with a primary focus will be to create transformational learning communities fiercely committed to educational equity and excellence for women worldwide. The need to provide leadership and expertise to assess, identify, formulate, and implement a mission that will serve millions, goals, and objectives to make equity and inclusion a reality. Main key is an Inclusive Culture to spreading your message to millions. One way to make inclusion a reality is to collaborate with women around the world and model an open dialogue around race, culture, class, and other issues of differences. We must find what works and doesn't work by finding and researching best practices, innovations, and research across multiple disciplines and subject areas. We must understand historical contexts and the active investment in changing social structures and practices over time. Create a common vocabulary and protocol for resource allocation and evaluating strategic investments. Just having a seat at the table is not inclusion. It is finding your voice and sharing your message that creates a more Inclusive Culture. Dr. B. stepped into her greatness when she found her voice, responsibility, and duty to the world that helps you and millions of women to share their Mission to Millions through her coaching programs, publishing books for entrepreneurs, Dr. B app, and B-Global masterminds & business ventures. Visionary Leaders should strive toward optimal inclusion to create a strong community, strong connections, giving people a sense of belonging.

Strategies to Succeed in Our COVID Changed World

Dr. B. often says that COVID-19 might have kept us home and stopped the local connections, but it opened an internet portal to connect with the world. During COVID-19 the world shut down and for a minute the world froze; however, immediately we found a solution that has changed the way we did things. One of Dr. B's giant steps during COVID-19 was connecting with women around the world and creating PowerTalk Livestream where she interviews people from all over the world so they can share their message. Innovation is another recipe to spreading your Mission to Millions. Use the internet, get on Podcast, or create your own, use online TV such as Apple TV or Amazon Fire TV. If it doesn't exist, invent it. You have a greater being within you that has the confidence and power to achieve your big dreams. Dr. B. believes in you. You should believe in yourself too! Believing in yourself is a vital key you must use and use again in your Million to Millions journey because if you don't no one else will. Dr. B coaches you on how to write a book, turn it into an e-course, and shows you how to get a speaking gig so you start to share your Mission to Millions.

Author's quote

"Greatness is a lifelong mission. Create a mission to serve millions and, gently with love, shake the world."
Dr. B

To win people's hearts more easily, we must be kind, compassionate, and authentic. We can attract more flies with honey. To serve millions of people, we must lead with a clear mission. Vishen Lakhiani says, "The most extraordinary people in the world today don't have a career. They have a mission." A mission to millions is a life mission, remember this important key to Mission to Millions. It is not a career. It is your passion and life' s purpose. It is a sense of responsibility bigger than you to serve. Create a mission to serve millions and, gently with love, shake the world. To gain a better understanding of how to create a Mission to Millions book that is being published soon. You can also sign up to the Mission to Millions coaching program and B-Global Business Ventures and Masterminds, see QR codes below to gain more information.

Bio

Dr. Angelica Benavides is known as Dr. B and the Ultimate Legacy Builder. She increases visibility, exposure, and influence, helping entrepreneurs be all they can be. Dr. B's, [Angélica Benavides (Underwood) Ed.D.] story is being written and shared worldwide by the Women's World Conference and Awards. She has been featured on NBC, USA Today, Fox and recognized as an Amazing Women of Influence. She shared a Global Virtual Stage with Forbes Riley, Bill Walsh, Ragne Sinikas, and Dr. Freddy Behin.

Dr. B's certifications are in Associate in Arts, Bachelor of Interdisciplinary, Master of Science, Doctoral Leadership with a Specialization in Curriculum & Instruction. These don't define her but shape who she is now. Dr. B has always been curious about Learning Theories, Human Development, and how the brain functions. She dedicated a decade to researching and discovering how humans learn, develop, and how we can shift our beliefs to shift our decision-making and actions.

Dr. B has learned from the giants such as Anthony Robbins, Dean Graziosi, John Maxwell, Grant Cardone, Forbes Riley, Bill Walsh, Mark Victor Hansen to help her think bigger, make bigger decisions, and take giant action steps toward her mission to millions. She now creates even more success for businesswomen owners. Dr. B specializes in publishing books, business programs, speaker training programs, certification programs, and global masterminds. She puts on the table the best resources that every business needs to learn about to survive and thrive in any economy. You will love her message as she always delivers cutting-edge content.

Dr. Angelica Benavides is known as Dr. B. She inspires women worldwide to share their Mission to Millions and their stories. She is a Badass Influencer, an Ultimate Legacy Builder, A World-Class Storyteller, Best-Selling Author, Serial Entrepreneur, and Publisher.

You have a special talent, a gift to be shared that will influence those it touches. Storytelling is an important social aspect of life, and your life should be remembered.

Dr. B is the Marketing Director, Advisory Board Member, and Publisher for Face of Women of Heart Awards (WOHA) for 2021. She was recently invited to the International Advisory Board for the 100 Successful Women in Business Network.

Learn more about this author

"...it is sad, of course, to forget. But it is a lonely thing, to be forgotten. To remember when no one else does." — V.E.

What I Offer:

- Book Collaborations to Gain More Visibility and Exposure World-Wide
- Publish your book without hiring a ghostwriter
- Build strong connections and find the right strategies with Dr. B. Elite Mastermind & Ventures
- K-12 Online Academy for youth around the world leading them to Entrepreneur Career Path

- and much more...

We give up to 10% of the net to the Alive and Beautiful Breast Cancer Association.

Conclusion

by María Angélica Benavides, EdD

T he 20 phenomenal women in this book have come a long way. You are probably feeling overwhelmed and thinking I have too much chaos. These women had many challenges, but they took those challenges and polished them by learning from their experience. They talk their walk and are paving the way for you to reach greatness. It is not easy to shine because we have been programmed to follow the rules and be good girls and boys on a command-based system. We were penalized for thinking outside the box. We remind you that you were born to be great. We all have the best version of ourselves inside. Life challenges carve, shape, and polish us into who we have become. Who do you choose to be, average or great? Greatness is not a destination but a journey that you become wiser, braver, bolder, and brings clarity to your whole being at every phase of life. We hope that the idea of greatness is not intimidating for you anymore. Greatness must be intentional and aligned in all areas of your life: health, education, relationships, business, and spirituality. "I am." Dare to be great! Dare to be YOU!

Once you gain a bigger vision, you become a visionary leader because you are ready to impact and make a difference to millions. We don't know why you are reading the book right now. We hope you are preparing to share your vision with many. You are probably a visionary leader already and need to boost other visionary leaders just like you. Whatever the reason for reading this book is perfect. We are in the right place, have the right mindset, and are ready for the next great thing. If so, go for that big dream. If you are waiting for perfection, there is no such thing. All experts are always students first; we all need help and support in life. Glad you picked up this book. A visionary leader can discover their greatness within when they have the right mindset, strategies, and resources.

The next step is to connect with all the authors in this book. Join their community or simply reach out and tell them how this book impacted or shaped your thinking. Let's encourage each other to keep going. Buy more books to give to other women who need to be inspired, motivated, and encouraged to discover their greatness within. Do you know a visionary leader that is ready to step into their greatness? If you are in a corporate world, invite an author to speak to your leaders. We want to activate more leaders and help them come alive to serve more and do more in business, life, and the world.

Remember,

"Where there is no vision, the people perish." - Proverbs 29:18

Learn more about this author

Venture With Dr. B.

Citations

Coombs, S. (2020, April 13). Show Me, Don't Tell Me…words vs actions. Retrieved December 10, 2021, from Samcoombs.medium.com Website https://samcoombs.medium.com/words-are-c57be5863dd4

Dreamtime. (2021). Map of the world on face of girl. Retrieved February 12, 2021) from www.dreamstime.com

EcoWatch. (2017, June 29). Jane Goodall's Vision for the Future. Retrieved January 4, 2021, from Ecowaaatch.com Website https://www.ecowatch.com/jane-goodall-video-

English Standard Bible, (n.d), Colossians 3:23

English Standard Version Bible, 2001, Proverbs 29:18

Fernandez, C. (2020, May 8). 28 Michelle Obama Quotes That Will Inspire You to Live Your Best Life. Oprah Daily. Retrieved December 28, 2021. From OprahDaily.com Website https://www.oprahdaily.com/life/relationships-love/g25438427/michelle-obama-quotes/

Farrer-Brown, M. (2020, September 20). How does an Emotionally Fit leader go about their day? Retrieved December 9, 2021. From fittolead.net website https://fittolead.net/how-does-an-emotionally-fit-leader-go-about-their-day/

Gilligan, C. (1982). In a Different Voice: Psychological Theory and Women's Development. Harvard University Press.

Goalcast (n.d.). 25 Maya Angelou Quotes to Inspire Your Life. Retrieved January 20, 2021, From Goalcast.com Website https://www.goalcast.com/maya-angelou-quotes-to-inspire-your-life

Grady, C. (2019, July 30). Why Marianne Williamson's most famous passage keeps getting cited as a Nelson

Mandela quote. Retrieved January 24, 2022, from Vox.com Web Site:
https://www.vox.com/culture/2019/7/30/20699833/marianne-williamson-our-deepest-fear-nelson-mandela-return-to-love

Hochschild, A.R., Emotion Work, Feeling Rules, and Social Structure. (Nov. 1979). American Journal of Sociology, Vol. 85(3), pp. 551-575. Published By: The University of Chicago Press

Inspiring Quotes. (2022). Jean Houston Quotes and Sayings. Retrieved January 9, 2022, from inspiringquotes.us Website https://www.inspiringquotes.us/author/4412-jean-houston

Judy Garland Quotes. (n.d.). BrainyQuote.com. Retrieved January 24, 2022, from BrainyQuote.com Web site: https://www.brainyquote.com/quotes/judy garland 104276

Leader Quotes. (n.d.) Best quotes by Luvvie Ajayi on World. Retrieved December 10, 2021, from leaderquotes.org website https://leaderquotes.org/best-quotes-by-luvvie-ajayi-on-world.html

Lucas, D. (2017, August 17). Leadership Series. CredoFinance.com. Retrieved December 20, 2021, from https://credofinance.com/great-leaders-give-people-vision-bigger-week-32/

Mani, M. (2019, April 24). Maya Angelou Butterfly Quote To Inspire You. Retrieved January 24, 2022, from outofstress.com Web site https://www.outofstress.com/we-delight-in-the-beauty-of-the-butterfly-maya-angelou-quote/

Monroe, S. (November 30, 2020). Bold. https://medium.com/be-bold/my-mission-in-life-is-not-merely-to-survive-but-to-thrive-and-to-do-so-with-some-passion-some-996523b1b2fa

Napoleon Bonaparte. (n.d.). AZQuotes.com. Retrieved January 24, 2022, from AZQuotes.com Web site: https://www.azquotes.com/quote/1057418

Pierron, J. (2020, November 29). Book Review - The Invisible Life of Addie LaRue. Retrieved January 3, 2022, from jesspierron.com Web site: https://jesspierron.com/the-invisible-life-of-addie-larue/

Philosiblog. (2015, September 3). The only thing worse than being blind is having sight but no vision. Retrieved January 8, 2022, from philosiblog.com Web site: https://philosiblog.com/2015/09/03/the-only-thing-worse-than-being-blind-is-having-sight-but-no-vision/

Princess Diana Quotes. (n.d.). BrainyQuote.com. Retrieved January 24, 2022, from BrainyQuote.com Web site: https://www.brainyquote.com/quotes/princess_diana_154337

Robin S. Sharma Quotes. Quotefancy.com. Retrieved December 18, 2020, from quotefancy.com Web site: https://quotefancy.com/quote/953706/Robin-S-Sharma-Leadership-is-less-about-the-position-you-hold-than-the-influence-you-have

Satara, A. (n.d). 1 Oprah Quote All Good Entrepreneurs Should Live ByIf it works for Oprah it will work for you. Retrieved January 22, 2022, from inc.com Web site: https://www.inc.com/alyssa-satara/oprah-sums-up-how-entrepreneurs-can-stay-determined-in-a-few-brief-sentences.

Scipioni, J. (2020, February 12). Michelle Obama: Why going 'high' when faced with a challenge is so important to her. Retrieved January 20, 2021, from CNBC.com make it Web site: https://www.cnbc.com/2020/02/12/michelle-obama-on-famous-catchphrase-when-they-go-low-we-go-high.html

Smithsonian National Museum of African Art, 2022. Heroes Principles of African Greatness. Retrieved January 5, 2022, from Web site:

https://africa.si.edu/exhibitions/current-exhibitions/heroes-principles-of-african-greatness

Tots' N Tutors. (20221, May 12). Educational Inspiration: 25 Quotes. Retrieved January 6, 2022, from totsntutors.com Web site: https://totsntutors.com/teaching-in-austin/

The White House. (2016, March 8). Remarks By The First Lady at Let Girls Learn Event Celebrating International Women's Day. Retrieved January 9, 2022, from obamawhitehouse.archieves.gov. Website https://obamawhitehouse.archives.gov/the-press-office/2016/03/08/remarks-first-lady-let-girls-learn-event-celebrating-international

Turner, N. (2019, January 10). A Passport to the Future. Retrieved January 2, 2022, from RaisingSupaman.com Web Site: https://raisingsupaman.com/2019/01/a-passport-to-the-future/

Woodall, T. (2015, August 5). QOD-036: Maya Angelou – People will never forget how you made them feel. Retrieved December 15, 2020, from Goal Getting Podcast Web site: http://www.goalgettingpodcast.com/qod-036-maya-angelou-people-will-never-forget-how-you-made-them-feel/

Manufactured by Amazon.ca
Bolton, ON

24164105R00144